ARTIFICIAL RELIGION

--- ❧ ---

NEVILLE WILLIAMS

Trafford rev. 07/01/2016

 www.trafford.com

North America & international
toll-free: 1 888 232 4444 (USA & Canada)
fax: 812 355 4082

PREFACE

The first section of the book follows a video produced by Richard Dawkins with the title "The God Delusion." Dawkins explores the unproven beliefs that are treated as factual by many religions, and the extremes to which some followers have taken them. He argues that "the process of non-thinking called faith" is not a way of understanding the world, but instead stands in fundamental opposition to modern science and the scientific method, and is divisive and dangerous. The story began as a two–part documentary, (written and presented by Richard Dawkins), in which he argues that the world would be better off without religion. First broadcast in January 2006, in the form of two 45-minute episodes on Channel 4 (*in Britain*), The same investigation has also been presented as a series.

Richard Dawkins' interest in these matters took him into the dark places of this world, and led him to ask some difficult questions. He put himself 'in the picture,' and he seems to get the point across. And yet so many have watched and then just walked away and forgotten all about it.

I'm inviting you to read some of the material from the production and consider the outcome. The overall title for the work is fair, although it's more likely that others were involved in the naming process. By the time you have read through *this* material, I hope you will appreciate my suggested title, "A Dummies Guide to False Religion".

In the video—Richard Dawkins gives an adequate account of how 'they' appear to the outside world. My aim is to re–visit his material, and take an instruction book along for the ride, meanwhile trying to show that the religions of this world are really self-made; rather than 'real religions'— (following a real book).

One of the most obvious threats to the credibility of any religion is the fact that *there are hundreds of them*, as well as the different offshoots. Any reasonable person could see that if the things called churches were all following the same Book, they would each have a similar structure. For example they would each have the same position, (title) for the various levels of competence within their business. The present system has all sorts of names for their workers and all sorts of ideas about how things must be done. Also, to assume that the religions might have 'made up' some book (for their own benefit), would be utterly false, because they couldn't possibly have done a worse job, even if they tried. It simply wouldn't make any sense, for a religious organization to 'invent' a book that completely opposes their views, and their method of operation.

If you have already dismissed the book that I am referring to, you should at least agree that no good religion could ever develop from man made ideas. I hope you will come to see the difference, the vast **disconnect** between the Book and the end product (false–religion).

Regardless of where you now stand on religion you will soon come to realise that the various religions are proven to be *man-made*, and therefore cannot be built from their 'claimed' Instruction Book. The religions are simply using the Book as a leaning post, even using it as an excuse for their disgraceful behaviour.

In the future, humans will remove man-made religions from their education systems. When that time arrives please remember some of the points that are made in this book, to ensure you are on the side of truth.

Some things might seem difficult to cover. My main aim is to stick to the important topic, to get the message through to everyone. I find the stuff being taught in the name of religion to be a waste of time. Many students are learning things that have to be 'unlearned' at a later date. For example, students would need to unlearn the false, in order to take up a logical study of science. Students would need to unlearn the false, in order to just live a quite and peaceful life (after their education is complete). And worst of all, students would need to 'unlearn' the false in order to have any chance of understanding their Instruction Book.

Present day thoughts are often the result of long held views, (which is the very thing that needs to be cleared up). Matters concerning evolution and the work of Charles Darwin are not widely covered in this book. What is covered is an Instruction Book and how that book interacts with some of the views of science and opposes false religion. Matters concerning the science of Charles Darwin will be covered in a second book, with the title "Off The Hook."

I recognised at an early age, that there was something unique about The Instruction Book, from my own experience during my school years. I was challenged to "go look it up." So I toddled off with a scrap of paper, having a chapter name and some directions. I dusted off an old family Book and began to flick through it, looking for an exact chapter and verse, (to see what was really there). Then I heard others heading towards the room, I quickly turned the book over and sat a magazine on top. It seems I didn't want anyone to see me reading *that book.* When I thought about it later, it seemed quite strange. "Why was that one book so different from any other?"

If I had been reading any other book that day, say a history book, or a book of genealogy, or even a novel, I wouldn't have felt any stigma whatsoever. I realised that people like me were actually forbidding themselves from reading it. I began to wonder what kind of silent force was at work (inside my head) to make me feel that way. And why was it only *that book.*

As you read through you will see the same theme in almost every chapter. The poor old religionist doesn't stand a chance. Count how many times the Bible comes up with a different view when compared to the teachings of the fundamentalist religionist. If you are genuine you should be truly amazed. You should wonder how so many millions of people have owned a Bible without noticing the great hoax.

As soon as enough people come to realise the sheer waste involved in learning, and then unlearning, the false things in life, they may be able to work together to bring about an important (and much needed) change to our value system. Future action against religion will free–up student's time for studying something worthwhile.

Many of the quotes throughout are taken directly from Richard Dawkins work, which is available to watch on-line, with the title "The God Delusion" I hope you'll enjoy the parts of this book where Richard Dawkins hits them for six, by exposing the false nature of each 'invented' religion.

When reading any quoted text please consider the overall meaning, rather than concentrating on individual words. It will be difficult for you to overcome 'long held' views about a particular religious 'theme.' Please try to keep in mind that the matters raised in this book are NOT from my own imagination.

Many times throughout the book I talk about the difficult task of translating material from one language to another, so to help you realise the difficulty in translation, I have included some examples of modern day thoughts that were not exactly passed on the way they were intended.

Most of the following were taken from a leaflet produced by Air France (many years ago)…

A sign in a Bucharest motel…

THE LIFT IS BEING FIXED FOR THE NEXT DAY. DURING THAT TIME YOU WILL BE UNBEARABLE.

A sign in a Belgrade elevator…

TO MOVE THE CABIN, PUSH BUTTON FOR WISHING FLOOR. IF THE CABIN SHOULD ENTER MORE

PERSONS, EACH PERSON SHOULD ENTER A NUMBER OF WISHING FLOORS. DRIVING IS THEN GOING ALPHABETICAL BY NATIONAL ORDER.

A sign in a hotel in Athens...

VISITORS ARE EXPECTED TO COMPLAIN AT THE OFFICE BETWEEN THE HOURS OF 9:00 AND 11:00 DAILY.

A sign in a Yugoslavian hotel...

THE FLATTEN OF UNDERWEAR WITH PLEASURE IS THE JOB OF THE CHAMBERMAID.

A sign in a Japanese hotel...

YOU ARE INVITED TO TAKE ADVANTAGE OF THE CHAMBERMAID.

A sign in the lobby of a Moscow hotel, (near a monastery)

YOU ARE WELCOME TO VISIT THE CEMETARY WHERE FAMOUS RUSSIAN AND SOVIET COMPOSERS, ARTISTS AND WRITERS ARE BURIED DAILY, EXCEPT THURSDAY.

A sign outside a tailor shop in Hong Kong...

LADIES MAY HAVE A FIT UPSTAIRS.

A sign in a Bangkok dry cleaner...

DROP YOUR TROUSERS HERE FOR BEST RESULTS.

A sign in a laundry in Rome...

LADIES, LEAVE YOUR CLOTHES HERE AND SPEND THE AFTERNOON HAVING A GOOD TIME.

A sign in a Rhodes tailor shop…

ORDER YOUR SUMMER SUIT. BECAUSE IS BIG RUSH, WE WILL EXECUTE CUSTOMERS IN STRICT ROTATION.

A sign in a Zurich hotel…

BECAUSE OF THE INTIMACY OF ENTERTAINING GUESTS OF THE OPPOSITE SEX IN THE BEDROOM, IT IS SUGGESTED THAT THE LOBBY BE USED FOR THIS PURPOSE.

A sign in a Czech Tourist center…

TAKE ONE OF OUR HORSE-DRAWN CITY TOURS, WE GUARANTEE – NO MISCARRIAGES.

A sign at a Copenhagen ticket office…

WE TAKE YOUR BAGS
AND SEND THEM IN ALL DIRECTIONS.

A sign on the door of a Moscow hotel…

IF THIS IS YOUR FIRST VISIT TO USSR,
YOU ARE WELCOME TO IT.

A sign in a Japanese hotel.
(Above the air conditioner)…

COOLES AND HEATES:
IF YOU WANT JUST CONDITION OF WARM IN YOUR ROOM, PLEASE CONTROL YOURSELF.

THE WORK BEGINS

At the beginning of his work, Richard Dawkins introduces the theme of—"the elephant in the room"—yet this is so easily missed. It's quite easy to pass by that comment without even noticing. For me, *the elephant in the room* became apparent during the second viewing of the video.

He eventually continues with the following, "and in Britain even as we live in the shadow of holy terror, our government wants to restrict our freedom to criticise (religion). Science, we are told, should not tread on the toes of theology. But why should scientists tiptoe respectfully away? The time has come for people of reason to say, enough is enough, religious faith discourages independent thought, it's divisive and dangerous."

After the brief introduction—the main story begins with the mysterious world of religion. "If you want to experience the **medieval rituals** of faith, the candlelight, incense, music, important-sounding dead languages—nobody does it better than the Catholics. At Lourdes in Southern France the assault on the senses appeals to us, not to think, not to probe. And if we can retain our faith against the evidence, in the teeth of reality, the more virtuous we are."

At this point, I would interrupt proceedings to say, "We should all take a look at *their* Book, to see where *The Book* actually stands on these strange practices and medieval rituals." I commence with this world's well–known and much loved, annual tree–ceremony. Proving that the tree–ceremony is in fact a medieval 'left over' is really quite easy.

Starting with Jeremiah: Chapter 10 and verse 2.

Be not dismayed (at the signs of heaven); for the heathen are dismayed at them, for the customs of the people are vain: for one cuts a tree out of the forest, the work of the hands of the workman, (with an axe). They deck it with silver and with gold; they fasten it; that it move not." (KJV)

This is describing one of the ancient pagan rituals, an awful custom that was around *before* the modern churches, and was later adopted by them.

Disguised as a 'most popular holiday' the tree–ceremony is still practiced each year by the faithful followers (and non–followers alike). The "signs in the heavens"—that were frightening the superstitious—were in fact the onset of the winter solstice, the shortening of the hours (of sunlight). In *their mind* something needed to be done, to bring back the sunlight, to make their world safe from harm.

The Book, which they claim as their own, clearly informs the church *and the devoted followers* that such practices are vain (worthless), showing this annual 'high day' of the churches to be something to be avoided at all costs. One can plainly see from the text quoted that *anyone* who wants to continue to believe in the Book must not participate in this ridiculous ancient ritual. I challenge every reader to simply read it and believe what it says… "Learn–not the way of the heathen." That's fairly plain. Also, any person who considers themselves to be 'non-religious' (an atheist); should explain how they can be an atheist and (at the same time) take part in the most important (false) religious occasion of the year. Such a person is double-minded. A double minded person is unstable in all his ways.

We have already seen that Richard Dawkins has exposed the false nature of religious ceremonies. There is much more to cover about the un-natural event described above. However, at this stage it is more important to stick with the story as provided by Richard Dawkins.

Rather than complete the story of Molech and Sandy Claws (at this stage)––I will give a brief description of the remainder of the first part of this book, then on to the weird and wonderful fairy-story about the Catholic Mary.

Most of the first section expands on the work done by Richard Dawkins. There are many other mysterious and opposing views covered. Truthful things are covered, that most people would expect are simply not found in the Bible. The various false religions of this world have done a thorough job of deceiving the masses, yet the actual text exposes their counterfeit ideas. Some readers may have the opinion that my book provides a "free ride" for science–versus–religion, try to keep in mind that the praises of science are for (*all the parts of science that are truthful and accurate.*)

This book gives a tick of approval to any scientist anywhere who is willing to tell the truth about the absurd nature of the religious organizations of this world.

Congratulations to Richard Dawkins for his effort in exposing the great disconnect between what the religions are supposed to do, and what they actually do. The point is this, if there is such a thing as a "true church" in this world, it will be the one that actually reads (and follows) The Instruction Book.

At this stage I have only covered a few minutes of the first video, and I am keen to move on to the next part. However right now, a brief summary of what's to come would be more helpful.

My second chapter shows that Mary, as depicted in the Bible, is actually asleep in the ground to this day, and cannot possibly be doing any of the churchy things that are promoted by various Sunday religions.

In the third chapter, Dawkins shows that many religions believe in a 'young Earth'– approx. 6000 years old. He then goes on to show evidence that supports a planet that is clearly billions of years old. I intend to show that the Bible–story could not possibly support the idea of a young Earth. In fact if you can find an older copy of the Bible you will see that there is a break between each of the verses. Right from the get–go, the process of joining verse one and verse two into a paragraph distorted the story (and supported a particular world–view). In fact the missing years occur between two verses, and there is plenty of evidence to support this. The very first verse is not intended as the beginning of the universe or even as the beginning of planet Earth, it points to a time when the Earth first became useful (for life). The time between verse one and verse two is not covered because it would require hundreds of books. Besides, the Bible is intended to be an Instruction Book for mankind, not a story of how the Earth changed from a state of great beauty to a state of chaos. Please keep in mind that this is not some weird idea of mine. I didn't invent some fantastic story just to make myself sound intelligent, all I did was read The Book to see for myself what it really said about these events.

The fourth chapter is really one that could be skipped. However if Richard Dawkins or any atheist scientist ever reads the fourth chapter he may benefit a little, by noticing that he really needs to follow this advice. Get rid of some of the gods from your life. Start by scrapping the ancient 'religious' customs that you participate in each year. What about you; are you telling your friends or relatives that these religious occasions are ancient and mysterious and silly, and yet continuing with these same traditions with your own family?

In chapter five the story follows the indoctrination of children. Surely, if the various religions are using the same book, then they'll all be the same, or at least very similar. The reason for any religion to grab the children early must be to prevent them from learning some other false religion. On the other hand, if they were working together in a spirit of co-operation then it wouldn't matter where the young ones were taught. In a real world--where religions all teach the same message--from the same book, it simply wouldn't matter where their early training occurred.

In chapter six, Dawkins recommends a good strong dose of rational thinking. Some religious groups think they can save children--by scaring the daylights out of them. Of all the wrong ideas in the world of religion, this would have to be the most bizarre. They have 'dreamed up' a strange place where humans are tormented--apparently forever. I assure you, if there were such a terrible place, these clowns would be the first customers. The Bible itself does NOT support this 'man–made' idea of hell and torment.

Chapter seven is about a person who takes it upon himself to murder a fellow human being. If you read through the whole story, you will find once again, that Dawkins and the Bible are in agreement. No one has the right to judge another human for any reason. No one has the right to decide that someone should be murdered.

Chapter eight uncovers the idea of the man–kind being closely related to the chimp-kind, "just like windows–2000 is closely related to the computer software known as Ms-dos." I ask the question... "Can you think of anything that the computer had going for it, that the chimp couldn't possibly have had?"
The end of chapter eight coincides with the end of the work of Richard Dawkins (the film). The closing chapters of my book then fill in some details, including the fascinating story of 'The Pathfinder of the Seas.'

For now it is sufficient for you to remember a point in your life where you considered the significance of a pagan ritual. An ancient ritual of cutting down a tree and fixing it in place, then decking it with silver and with gold, then (each year) sitting or kneeling down in front of it. The atheist will say, "It's not my religion, it's just tradition," lying to themselves and others about this awful and false practice.

The fundamental religionist will say, "It is just a harmless tradition." Well perhaps they believe that God's Book is just having a little joke, when it plainly says, "Learn not the way of the heathen."

Yes I'm still trying to move on to chapter 2… But, for those who will never buy my book I have included my own credentials, so you can begin to understand what sort of qualifications are needed for a proper understanding.

The following statement is repeated at the end of the book.

My final comment is very plain and clear, there is
no wriggle room at all, so before I go there, I'd like
to take the time to cover my own credentials.

What right do I have to read and understand
The Instruction Book? Or, what sort of person would qualify
as a candidate for reading and *understanding* the truth?

Gal. 6:3

For if a man think himself to be something,
when he is nothing, he deceives himself.

Luke 14:11

For whoever exalts himself shall be abased;
and he that humbles himself shall be exalted.

1 Cor. 3:18

Let no man deceive himself.
If any man among you seems to be wise in this world,
let him become a fool, that he may be wise.

My first 'full-time' job was with Telecom Australia, known as 'Postmaster–Generals Department.' [I came sixth in the state (in the entrance exam).]

I didn't get that job, yet I have been hounded all my life to "go out and get a real job." The reasons for not getting my first job are simple and straightforward... (just like me).

This is how my doctor's certificate reads...
And these are the reasons why an 'Australian Government department' rejected me as a fellow human being. And yes, they are still hounding me to 'get a job'––to this day.

·   He has defective vision.
·   He is underweight for his age. (poor physique)
·   He has a history of asthma.

So you see, I am foolish and weak;
I am a simpleton, and a blockhead.

And there are plenty of folks in my local area who can back that up!

Now back to the story (as presented)...

Chapter Two

MARY SLEEPS

The following section of the film takes a look at the wonder associated with Mary. The video goes on to show the faithful followers gathering at a (religious) site. (6:52)

"Daylight reveals more of this shrine, where a myth is perpetuated that a virgin who gave birth, Christ's mother Mary, appeared here once to an impressionable young girl.

The faithful make the pilgrimage here because they believe that terrible afflictions can be cured, by dragging their poor bodies up to a pool of water, (where Mary supposedly made her miraculous appearance)."

Then follows; "Religion is about turning untested belief into unshakeable truth through the power of institutions and the passage of time. Catholics believe that Mary was so important that she didn't physically die, instead her body shot–off into heaven when her life came to a natural end, of course there's no evidence for this. Even the Bible says nothing about how Mary died."

Here we have arrived at an important point—the very thing that most people have overlooked. The words above should grab your attention. This is the part where he points out that there is a huge discrepancy between the Book, (which the religions claim to follow), and their actual religious beliefs. **"Even the Bible says nothing about the way Mary died."** The belief that her body was lifted into heaven emerged about six centuries after Jesus' time.

"Made up, like any tale and spread by word of mouth. But it became established tradition. It was handed down over centuries. The odd thing about tradition is that the longer it's been going, the more people seem to take it seriously. It's as though the sheer passage of time makes something––that to begin with was just made up–– turn into something that people believe as factual."

He then goes on to explain how that tradition became a decree that Roman Catholics *must* now believe. To consider this belief thoroughly, the following questions must be considered.

Did Mary float on up to heaven when she died?

Is it appropriate to pray to Mary as a mediator?

The Book provides some simple answers (as follows). Keep in mind, words recorded in the Book (whether real or otherwise) cannot be later removed or disregarded, changes cannot be 'back dated' to suit some man–made ideal. You should be able to see how silly the idea becomes, by considering my exaggerated story about the men who were buried in the tombs.

Acts: 1:14.
These all continued with one accord in prayer and supplication, with the women, and Mary the mother of Jesus, and with His brothers—In this verse we see that no one was praying to Mary, she was their equal.

Also—Matthew: 2:11.
And when they were come into the house, they saw the young child with Mary (his mother), and fell down, and worshipped <u>Him</u>.

Did Mary float on up to heaven at any time?

Job 14:10.

But man dies, and wastes away, man gives up the human spirit, and where *is* he? *As* the waters fail from the sea, and the flood decays and dries up: So man lies down, and rises not, they shall not awake, (not raised out of their sleep). The truth from the past leaves little doubt.

1 Thessalonians 4:16

For the Lord himself shall descend from heaven with a shout, with the voice of the archangel, and with the trump of God: and the dead in Christ shall rise first (**future**).

1 Corinthians 15:22

For as in Adam all die, even so in Christ shall all be made alive. But every man in his own order: Christ the first–fruits; afterward they that are Christ's **at His return.**

Note the part where it plainly states "at his return;" that is not an optional extra; it refers to an event that has not yet occurred.

From the quotes given, it is easy to see, that Mary would be better off sleeping, just like all humans who have ever died, rather than ending up in the wrong place at the wrong time!

(Could Mary be a mediator)?

I Timothy 2:5.

There is one God and one mediator between God and mankind.

The Book claims a total of one mediator and then names Him; so what can religion do with that plain statement. How can they make that go away? Mary (as a mediator) would simply be one too many.

Almost everyone has heard of "The Lord's Prayer." In the first few verses it plainly states the words "on Earth" (as it is in Heaven). The original Mary loved to learn; so she would have known the verse and would be hoping to see God's kingdom, "on Earth;" (at some future time), Mary would not have wanted to be floating around in space, or in some other dimension if she was praying; "Thy Kingdom come, thy will be done, on Earth…"

Just getting off the track a little here… The above verse also shows that God's will is NOT being done here on Earth at the present time.

Another serious problem (for the truth) is the timing of the events. We can see that there was a time when there was one thing special about Mary. (She was blessed––because she was the mother of Jesus). Then a later time, when she was believed to have floated on up to heaven; then a time when that new **idea** became "official."

So, would you please consider this imaginary conversation between the early self–made pope and the author of the Bible.

Something like this perhaps; "Well we sort of told everyone that You will forget all that 'sleep in the dust' stuff, and go dig up Mary's bones and have her floated–on–up–to–heaven. Oh, by the way, could you back–date the float–on–up–to-heaven part (to suit the fairy story that we have made up)."

If we can get past such obvious nonsense (from the church) and accept the idea that Mary sleeps––to this day; then the question arises, "Who is this Catholic–Mary?" or "Where did she come from?"

What about the story of the men in the tombs? If all of the above isn't enough to convince you, there is the story of the men who were raised from the dead. (This occurred shortly after an earthquake late on the Wednesday afternoon.

Matthew 27:52.
The tombs broke open; the bodies of many holy people who had died were raised to **physical life.**

First, grasp that these dead bodies were raised to life they were not raised to anywhere else, other than to life as a human. that is very plain. It's also important to grasp that these dead bodies did not shoot off to heaven at the time of death, yet they were described as "holy men."

Now (just for fun) let's try to cover the above story in a way that will support the Catholic idea of floating off to heaven.

First we would assume that these other holy people had 'shot off to heaven' when *they* died. Then, on this very special Wednesday afternoon, the following events would have to occur.

These poor fellows would have to be dragged back down from 'heaven,' then killed off all over again, then shoved back in the tombs, and then finally resurrected to life on Earth; (to fulfill verse 52).

If you are willing to think this through, it's easy to see what a load of old rubbish is being peddled by the floating–off–to–heaven church. The truth is; Mary sleeps in the earth. Any other idea, whether fashionable or not, simply makes a mockery of all the Bible stories!

Chapter Three

THE EARTH BECAME VOID

The next section of Dawkins' work focuses on the age of the Earth itself. Comparing religious beliefs with accepted science, (such as the fossil record). You might be inclined to see this as simply another 'advertisement for evolution'. Please think back to the introduction, this work is not about promoting 'the theory of evolution'; it is about *the elephant in the room* (false religion). Another point I would like to make, is that evolution, (in the mind of the hardened atheist) is not under any threat from religion, as you can see from the following important message.

"Even if all the data point to a designer, such an hypothesis is excluded from science because it is not naturalistic."

The statement above applies to all scientists, (anyone with the good letters after their name).

But for those of the man—kind, you should be able to drag your head down out of the cloud of science, and think for yourself. And what is the first thing you will easily notice, (once you are free from the call of science)?

Well, the very first thing you will notice is that every item in the scientific "tree of life" is a FINISHED PRODUCT (or a small part belonging to a finished product)! The only intermediates are bits of bones that won't fit into one pile or the other, but they are all from a finished product of some 'kind.'

Even the tiniest micro–organism is a finished product, with all the right parts, and in all the right places. And some of these have been around for hundreds of millions of years!

Anyway, the point being made (by Dawkins) is that, the religions of this world promote the idea of a 'young Earth'—an impossible place created instantly—and only a few thousand years ago, which of course flies in the face of scientific evidence. Dawkins points out that the fundamental religionist believes that the book of Genesis describes a designer who fashioned the Earth in just six days. I hope (after filling in the detail) the reader will easily see that this religious theme is just another counterfeit.

To complete this chapter properly, I would need to commence with a great deal of material taken from different parts of the Book, (here a little—there a little) as instructed. I would also need to delve into various definitions of words and phrases, however with that approach you may lose interest. For the benefit of the reader I have taken a step back from the detail, to give a plain statement of what the first verses actually portray. I have then taken another step to give the all–important *timing* of these events.

You should consider that the earlier versions of the Book (before the translation to English), would have been much more obvious in the meaning, certain words and meanings were 'lost in translation.' The workers already had a world–view; (they 'knew' what it was all about), and they would have been under pressure to 'get–it–right,' (whatever 'right' may happen to be).

In the Book of Genesis, the first verse and the second are about two different 'times.' *Neither* verse refers to the beginning of time (the big bang). Also, if you have an interest in the beginning of time; I can recommend "A Brief History of Time" by Stephen Hawking; it's a terrific story (and easy to follow). So the following, finally, is the truthful account.

The first verse refers to an era that began billions of years ago, (when the Earth was made beautiful and ready for occupation). **The second verse** refers to another era that began thousands of years ago, (after the Earth had decayed into a hostile environment, unfit for physical life).

You may be thinking—"how on earth could he work that out?" Well I say to you, read the information that I have provided (from the Instruction Book) and then think—"how on earth could it be read and understood any other way?" This is plain text, it is available for all to read, even the fundamental religionist.

Verse one: Describes the beginning of the process of generating an atmosphere on Earth for the first time. (See notes about "shawmayim" *the arch in which the clouds move*).

Verse two: Describes a time, much later when the Earth had decayed into a state of chaos, covered by an atmosphere that was fouled (and spinning out of control), a time when the whole Earth was covered in darkness.

The book doesn't say, verse one—followed by a gap of billions of years—then verse two, however getting these two verses right is the only way to make sense of the rest of The Book. There is much more to be explained here; try to keep in mind that I am **not** trying to prove that I'm reading from some kind of science text–book. I am simply trying to show that anyone who takes a simple approach— without any preconceived ideas—can find a different meaning, (very different to what they have learned from others).

The key to verse one is found by looking up the original Hebrew word for '**the heavens**' shamayim {shaw-mah'-yim}'dual' of an unused 'singular' **shameh** {shaw-meh'}; *from an unused root meaning to be lofty; the sky (as aloft; the dual perhaps alluding to* **the visible arch in which the clouds move, as well as to the higher ether where the celestial bodies revolve**). (Also try to keep in mind that the definition given has been around for thousands of years).

Popular opinion assumes that the people from BC should be labeled as 'Flat–Earth–people,' yet the Hebrew language envisaged 'a higher ether' as well as 'revolving celestial bodies.' It is important to note that there were a lesser number of words in the vocabulary in ancient times, and therefore words had different meanings, and the meaning was found in the context of what was being written. For that reason the term heaven is often used to refer to the Earth's atmosphere (and sometimes the entire universe).

For verse two the key to understanding relies on simple words like "was" and "void" and so on.

I'll start with void (because that's an easy one to discuss). Many readers over the years have assumed that 'void' meant non–existent, but you can see that it really means used–up. An example would be an old, thick–cardboard railway ticket, (once used for country rail travel). When a passenger reached the final destination an attendant would punch–through, with the word 'VOID,' (so the ticket wouldn't be used again). As you can see, that didn't mean that the ticket had never existed, merely that it was now unusable. And so it was for planet Earth, it had simply become unusable.

Now for the tough one "was", The Hebrew word used is "hayah {haw-yaw}" **to exist**, i.e. **to become** or **come to pass.**

So if we show the verse differently (using the original meaning) we see, 'and the Earth **became**'—in place of—and the Earth was. Again I say, very little effort was required to make sense of the original text *as it was intended.*

Along with the translations given, there needs to be just a little more evidence. I want to prove from The Book that the first verse describes a much earlier time.

Understanding the remainder of the first few pages will hinge on a simple use of the word 'after' so it should be easy, but first some obvious differences between the two eras.

The beginning of the book of John looks back to an earlier time, making it a good place to start the explanation. John's words also clearly show that there were **two** beings, in the God family, which should be a wake–up call for those studying a triune; or 'trinity being.' (Again, one too many, or perhaps one short, depending on which way you contrive *three beings in the one place*). Sounds like the idea of a mad–man!

John 1:1. In the beginning was the Word and the Word was with God, and the Word was God. The same was in the beginning with God; all–things were made by Him; and without him was not anything made (KJV).

Now we know that a few sentences, no matter how plain, can cause confusion, but that need not be.

The name used is a **family name.** For example suppose a man's surname was Smith and his son's name was Bill Smith and the two of them designed and built a useful device (while working together as a family). You would be able to write—"In the beginning was Bill; and Bill was with Smith; and Bill was Smith; and he was with Smith from the beginning.

For two beings to design and print the base matter for a three dimensional universe they would have to already exist in another "place," (perhaps a fifth dimension). As humans, we may only *contemplate* the first and second dimension (but we can never see it). It would be silly for science to deny the existence of the second dimension, just because 2D 'objects' will always be invisible. For one thing we need to use 2D calculations to figure out where a star might be in 3D space. So given that we believe in the second dimension, it must be 'ok' for science to accept the idea of a fifth dimension as well, (as long as it contains no living being, of course).

In other words the family of two, described above, would have already existed in a place where time (as we know it) was not that critical, (mainly because it hadn't started yet).

The bible timeline clearly has the Earth already in existence for billions of years, before it was made beautiful.

And billions of years later it became 'void.' So The Book of John describes an even earlier time, and The Book of Job speaks of the Earth, later, (Again, the time mentioned in verse one).

The following is a question asked of a man named Job, it seems at first to be confusing; and even a tad far-fetched, until someone is willing to apply some critical thinking. Job 38:5. Question; "Who has laid the measures thereof, if you know? Or who has stretched the line upon it? Whereupon are the foundations thereof fastened? Or who laid the corner stone. When the morning stars sang together and all the sons of God shouted for joy?" (KJV).

This is a question put to Job in a language that *he* could understand, Job knew it wasn't about a building–site. It was in fact a question about the Earth itself. The last part of the question doesn't seem to mean much, and yet there are three critical points to consider.

These 'stars' or 'angel beings' (millions of them) were individually created beings, (not male or female like the Man–kind), and shows that they were already in existence before the Earth was prepared for occupation.

They were **all** happy and in a state of **co-operation**, there was no deception at that time, and no liars.

The Earth, (when they **all** shouted for joy), must have been a finished product, and must have been pleasing to look at. In short, the Earth must have been made beautiful and ready to occupy, (not at all like the one described in verse two of Genesis)––Of course the above cannot be referring to the time of the 'big bang,' for obvious reasons.

This is getting even further off track, but how could you know that the angel–beings were sexless, manufactured beings? Matthew 22:23...(and this was a 'trick' question)...

The same day the Sadducees, (which say that there is no resurrection), asked him this, 'Moses said, If a man die, having no children, his brother shall marry his wife, and raise up children to his brother. Now there were with us seven brothers: and the first, when he had married a wife, deceased, and left his wife to his brother: Likewise the second, and the third, to the seventh. And last of all, the woman died also. Therefore in the resurrection whose wife shall she be of the seven? For they all had her.' Jesus answered and said to them; you are in error, not knowing the scriptures, or the power of God. For in the resurrection they neither marry, nor are given in marriage, but are as the angels from heaven.

[And the reason why the angels never marry is because they are neither male nor female].

What about the possibility of some 'being' actually making angel–beings? We need to stop and consider whether that is a 'far–fetched' claim; or is it something believable? I can imagine in early times, superstitious people simply wouldn't have had a chance to make sense of all that. But what about us, what about today's generation? Mankind can produce computer hardware, each one with its own serial number. We can produce various kinds of computer languages and software, each with its own serial number. We can 'pump out' these products by the millions, and think nothing of it. Try to imagine some book in the future, say thousands of years from now, a book that is making a claim about the millions of computers that mankind designed and produced. Would the reader of the future find such a task hard to believe? Yet we **have** achieved such a thing, (and we are mere humans living in the third dimension). Don't ever forget, humans **can** and do build computers by the millions and think nothing of it.

Of course there is much more to discover, but I believe that I have shown enough to distinguish between the ages. Before verse one: the universe. Before verse two, all the angels were in a state of co-operation. Between the verses—one third of them (the ones living on Earth)—changed into a permanent state of competition (opposition to their manufacturer). Many, many years before verse two the planet was in a beautiful state—ready to occupy. By the time described in verse two, the planet was in a state of chaos and covered in darkness.

Well, surely now you can see, it would take 'many books' to cover the events that must have occurred in that one 'space' between verse one and verse two. You can see that the Bible is not written for that time. It is written for our time. You can see that the real 'Instruction Book' could not possibly be twisted and distorted into something that supports a young–Earth theory. If your religious group is teaching a creation which occurred in only six thousand years, then you know they haven't been reading the same Book that

I have been reading, they have simply been learning and handing down a man–made religious belief.

The rest of the early pages describe the environmental recovery of the planet, (bringing it back from a state of chaos). When any reader sees or hears the word 'after' in general use it has a 'before' to go with it. For example: If I say "I will see you after lunch," you can assume the time of my speaking is 'before' lunch, and so on. The 'making' of plants and animals described in the early parts of Genesis, is actually a 're-printing' of 'the kinds' (one pair of the cat kind with complete instructions for all cats, one pair of the dog kind with complete instructions for all dogs, and so on, all built-in (pre-programmed). Made 'after' or like the 'kinds' that had once existed on Earth (in a different era). This is a claim of DNA technology. This is a claim of already understanding that a plant or animal has its own DNA (a blueprint for life). This re–making would seem far-fetched to superstitious peoples in the past—even a few hundred years ago—but what about this generation?

To give a comparison to human technology, it would be similar to storing samples of male and female DNA (usually in the form of blood) in a cryogenics lab, in the hope that some future scientist might be able to 're-make' one pair of the original 'kind' of creature. This form of technology is already available, and is being put to use by humans **at the present time.**

The rest of this story is fairly basic stuff. Once you discover that the word 'heavens' means either the atmosphere or; (in some cases) the universe; then the rest of Genesis begins to make a lot more sense. The light became visible when the thick dark atmosphere was cleared, (obviously an environmental improvement). The dividing of night from day would have required the return of the Earth's rotation to a twenty–four hour period, and so on. Such an effort is really not that hard to believe. You can be sure that if future scientists find a planet similar to Earth, they will figure out how to change certain aspects of the planet, in order to 'create' a more Earth–like environment.

Chapter Four

GO ONE FURTHER

Perhaps this chapter falls outside the area that I'm trying to cover. For the most part I'm using the fast–forward button on this part of the video.

I really should ignore pastor Ted altogether, but I must expose a few things. He's teaching the faithful followers that they were 'set free' from sin. I would simply say to him, please take a look at the book of 'Romans' before you start waffling on about being set free.

But what exactly is this weird thing called sin? Well, it simply means breaking one or more of the basic rules, (the laws) which are set in place.

1 John 3:4, explains this very simply…
"For sin is the transgression of the law."

There are laws about stealing or killing, laws about how to treat other people, even a law about taking a day off. Some rules are about 'what to do,' some are things 'not to do.' The average person would obey most of these laws, just by living a decent life, regardless of their belief system.

There are ten basic laws that should be taken seriously, so it should be fairly easy, right? Well apparently not! As you can see in

Romans: 3:23. For all have sinned, and come short of the glory of God; Romans 8:7; the human mind is enmity (hostile) against God; for it is *not* subject to the laws of God, neither indeed can be; and Romans 6:23; 'the wages of sin *is* death.'

I really don't think pastor Ted would be saying that *his* followers are set free, if he had actually read the Book. Or, perhaps he thinks his followers are above the law? Thank goodness the laws aren't as boring as pastor Ted!

The next part includes an atheist interviewing atheists, and more of the same old story of the continuing struggle between one form of religion and another. This is where I 'tune out,' so feel free to skip forward (as I did).

Then I reached a point in his story where Dawkins warns about "believing because you've been told to believe, rather than believing because you've looked at the evidence." Surely no one was expecting a solid, supporting comment from the Bible, yet here it is!

1Thes: 5:21.
Prove all things; hold fast that which is good.

Again that is not an option, even understanding (proving) The Book should be done with this rule in mind.

It simply means to look for further evidence, rather than jumping to conclusions, it can also mean, to be willing to let go of some of your "old fashioned" conclusions.

I see for a while in the video, there is nothing there for me to comment on, until I reach this point, which (for some) is the end of the first video.

"We are all atheists about *most* of the gods that societies have ever believed in, some of us just go one god further."

That statement is more relevant than you could imagine. Hopefully, after reading about some of the other mysterious unlawful customs, some readers, whether atheist or otherwise, will want to remove another god or two from their own lives.

Chapter Five

SEGREGATION

The remainder of the video–information was published separately with the title "The Virus of Faith."

Later on, when reading the story about Halloween you will see just how quickly 'the virus of faith' can spread, even into areas once free from contamination. In Australia, the virus of Halloween spread like wildfire and now (just a few years later) it is steamrolling its way through the whole community. It has now become a plague that cannot be stopped, and it happened in a country that had remained free of the virus for a very long time.

Halloween is an ancient Celtic ritual and has no place in Australian society, Halloween is wrong in any society. Children are taught to threaten homes and to "get something for nothing." That is not the Australian way.

In the next section of Dawkins work, we are taken through a dialogue about the separation of young children (into groups)— which are then taught a particular 'brand' of religion. Then taken through a question and answer scenario with a Jewish leader.

Richard Dawkins: "In this program I want to examine two further problems with religion. I believe it can lead to a warped and inflexible morality, and I'm very concerned about the religious indoctrination of children. I want to show how 'faith' acts like a virus that attacks the young and infects generation after generation."

"I want to ask whether **ancient mythology** should be taught in schools. It's time to question the abuse of childhood innocence with superstitious ideas of hell–fire and damnation. There is something exceedingly odd about the idea of sectarian religious schools. If we hadn't got used to it, (over the centuries), we'd find it downright bizarre."

"When you think about it, isn't it weird the way we automatically label a tiny child with its parents religion. Nobody would categorize children by the political party, which the parents support. We agree they're too young to know where they stand on questions of politics, so why is it not the same for where they stand on the cosmos, and humanity's place in it?"

"Children are initially separated from each other because of their parents faith, then their differences are constantly drilled into them, and they embark on opposing life trajectories. Such divisions are encouraged—not only in Israel, but right on [our] doorstep, in Northern Ireland for instance, or in London."

"In Northern London the Hasidic Community is the largest after Israel and New York. Here, religious division is taken to its extreme. Television is frowned upon, and of course children attend exclusive religious schools, clustered away from external influences—which just might persuade them to look outside their community. I want to find out why these children are being segregated, and whether their culture allows them to open their minds to reality."

The Book has more to say at this point, to repeat a message to the teachers of 'Judah' found in Matthew 23; "The Scribes and the Pharisees have the authority of Moses. All things then which they teach [from the book], do these and keep, but do not take their 'works' as your example, for they say—and do not. They make hard laws and put great weights on men's backs; *but they themselves will not put a finger to the task.* Notice the 'context,' (their works) represents the burdensome traditions, or the 'man–made' parts of their religion. So we can see from the simplicity of the Book, these clowns should stop making up their own sayings and go back to teaching the truth, regardless of their tradition!

Also; in Luke 13:34; O Jerusalem, Jerusalem, which killed the prophets, and stoned them that are sent; how often would I have gathered your children together, as a hen gathers her brood (under her wings), and yet you would not. The author of The Book wanted Judah to change their ways, (to *become* obedient), but they wouldn't.

Dawkins continues: "We live in the shadow of a religiously inspired terror, in an era when science has plainly shown religious superstition to be false. And yet it's a strange anomaly that 'faith–schools' are increasing in number and influence *in our education system*, with active encouragement from [Tony Blair's] government."

"There are already seven thousand faith schools in Britain and the government's trust reforms are encouraging many more. Over half the new city academies are (expected) to be supported by religious organizations. The most worrying development is a new wave of private evangelical schools that have adopted the American Baptist 'A.C.E.' curriculum (Accelerated "*Christian*" Education)."

Perhaps the correct words for 'A.C.E.' on this planet would be (Anti-Christian Education).

In the interview, this guy (Adrian) stumbled through the idea of the Earth being 'made' in six days. At least he was honest and said "I don't know," and then he went on to say, "it's a sort of an academic question really, and I don't care about the answer very much really. Does that make sense?"

I really don't need to waste any time on such a person! Adrian has a blank mind that would soak up any nonsense that was thrown his way. Anything that is, except the truth.

Dawkins continues: "But why should he impose his personal version of reality on children? Not only are they encouraged to consider the weird claims of the Bible; alongside scientific fact; they are also being indoctrinated into what an objective observer might see as a warped morality."

Here we see Dawkins associate 'the weird claims' with the Bible, however you should note that he has entered into this with his own world–view, (of how religion works). Richard Dawkins is kept busy with his own work as an evolutionary scientist, he simply doesn't have the time to consider the consequences of the vast disconnect that has occurred over the centuries, (even though he has hinted at it many times). What this clown (Adrian) believes, has got nothing to do with the Bible, and a whole lot to do with teaching what the people want, rather than learning and teaching the truth! Perhaps a better wording for the above is... [Not only are they encouraged to consider the weird claims of **false religion** alongside scientific fact, they are also being indoctrinated into what an objective observer might see as a warped morality.]

Dawkins: "Let me explain why, when it comes to children, I think of religion as a dangerous virus. It's a virus, which is transmitted partly through teachers and clergy, but also down the generations from parent to child to grandchild. Children are especially vulnerable to infection by the virus of religion. A child is genetically pre-programmed to accumulate knowledge from figures of authority. The child brain, for very good reasons, has to be 'set up' in such a way that it believes what it's told by its elders, because there just isn't time to experiment with warnings, like "don't go too near the cliff edge," or "don't swim in the river, there are crocodiles!" Any child who applied a scientific (questioning) attitude would be dead. No wonder the Jesuit said, "give me the child for his first seven years, and I'll give you the man."

"The child brain will automatically believe what it's told—even if what it's told is nonsense. And then when the child grows up, it will tend to pass on that same nonsense to its children."

Then he shows some more irrelevant material, (including a man with a loudspeaker). It may seem a little harsh, but in my opinion, anyone who takes a loudspeaker into a public place needs slapping!

Chapter Six

THE DARK PLACES

Dawkins: "For many people, part of 'growing up' is killing off the virus of faith, with a good strong dose of rational thinking. But if an individual doesn't succeed in shaking it off, his mind is stuck in a permanent state of infancy, and there is a real danger he will infect the next generation."

"I'm going to meet someone who has experienced 'religion as child abuse,' first hand. Jill Mytton was brought up in a strict 'christian' sect. Today she's a psychologist who rehabilitates young adults, similarly scarred by their narrow religious upbringing."

Jill Mytton: (London Metropolitan University);
"They need to be allowed to hear different perspectives on things. They need to be allowed to investigate. They need to be allowed to develop their critical faculties, so that they can take a number of different viewpoints and weigh them up, and decide which one is for them. They need to find their own pathway, not to be forced into a particular mold as a child. If I think back to my childhood, it's one that's kind of dominated by fear, and it was a fear of disapproval, while in the present, but also of eternal damnation."

"To a child, images of hell–fire and gnashing of teeth are actually very real and not metaphorical at all. If you bring a child up and discourage it from thinking freely, and making choices freely, then that's still (to me) that is a form of mental abuse, or psychological abuse."

Then, after a question on [hell], "It's strange isn't it, after all this time, it still has the power to effect me. This imaginary hell is a fearful place with torment and torture and it goes on forever, where there is no respite from it."

Dawkins: "It's deeply disturbing to think that there are 'believers' out there who actively use the idea of hell for moral policing. In the United States, 'christian' obsession with sin has spawned a national craze for 'hell–houses' (morality plays, come halloween freak shows), in which the evangelical 'hobby–horses' of abortion and homosexuality are literally demonised. Pastor Roberts is rehearsing a new production for his Colorado based hell–house, which he has written and staged for almost fifteen years. He fervently believes that you have to scare people into being good."

Pastor Keenan Roberts: "To call upon my life as a pastor, as a minister, *is to tell people what the book says*. And what I, and we, and our church, and hundreds of churches across this country, and around the world are doing is, we have found a very creative, effective tool that is getting people's attention, to consider the message. We want to leave an indelible impression upon their life, that sin destroys."

What he's really saying is that sin destroys, but you're not really destroyed, you're somehow kept alive? Meanwhile a message flashes on screen, which shows completely the opposite to what 'he' believes! Wouldn't you think that after fifteen years of reading, he would have had time to consider what that message plainly states? The message onscreen shows (in plain English) "The wages of sin is death." No amount of twisting and distorting, by these wannabe ministers, can turn that plain statement into something that supports their own personal 'invention,' their own 'false religion' or (as some call it) 'churchianity.' Put simply, death means death, not torment. Death has always been the same as sleep; it is a state of blackness and darkness.

At this point we need to clear up a few things about exactly what 'hell' is. What is the true definition, and what does the Instruction Book say, (about where people go when they die). Our English dictionary has all sorts of weird and wonderful ideas about "hell." However, such definitions come from a world–view, rather than from facts.

To see the true picture we need to look at the original word, as it was intended, as it was used, (in the Bible). That's really the only way to find the true meaning of the word. The word used in the Hebrew language was—showl; {sheh–ole}; which is defined as a grave or pit. Now let's look at a whole sentence that might have confused the ignorant, superstitious ministers of the past.

Psalms: 16:10:

You will not leave my soul in hell; neither will you suffer a holy one to see corruption. Here we see the words 'hell' and 'suffer' in the same sentence. Now let's take a look at the plain translation of the above, starting with the required Hebrew words and definitions. You should be ok with most of these words...(But what about the word... Soul—Hebrew: nephesh {neh'-fesh} properly, a breathing creature, i.e. animal of (abstractly) vitality; used very widely in a literal, accommodated or figurative sense (bodily or mental) any, appetite, beast, **body**, breath, creature.

[Obviously not something that could live forever in torment].

Hell–the **grave** or pit; (Very plain).

SUF"FER, v.t.[L. suffero; sub, under, and fero, to bear; as we say, to undergo.] . . .

3. To allow; to permit; not to forbid or hinder. Will you suffer yourself to be insulted?
[Webster's Revised Unabridged Dictionary (1828)]

Corruption: Hebrew: shachath {shakh'-ath} a pit (especially as a trap); figuratively **destruction**.

(For you will not leave my soul in hell; neither will you suffer your holy one to see corruption).

Now if we strip away the religious garbage, we can plainly see the written meaning in the text (as it was intended).

(The person referred to has overcome the world, and therefore qualified to be 'called.' To be raised to life).

Selected people; raised at the beginning of the next era, will not be at risk of the second death. While asleep there is no suffering, the dead sleep in–peace, hence the term "Rest In Peace." But to them, the time spent in the grave will **seem** like an instant, just as a good sleep seems to pass in an instant. Remember, all the garbage about hell comes from some religious freak in the distant past, and is definitely not supported in the Bible.

The false idea of suffering in 'hell,' follows on from the **false** idea of an immortal soul.

The Instruction Book plainly states that man *became* a living soul (body). It definitely does **not** say, man has an *Immortal* soul', it says he is a (living soul). The idea of an *immortal soul* must have been added by churchianity. Perhaps they thought it would be good for business, to offer the customers a cushy life in heaven, (in return for supporting their church). Anyway, the idea certainly did not come from The Book. So it is plain to see, that without an *immortal* soul, you're not going to suffer in hell and you're not going to 'float on up to heaven,' you are simply going to sleep. When you die, you will sleep in the dust of the Earth, as clearly stated so many times throughout The Book.

John: 11:11.

These things said he: and after that he said unto them, our friend Lazarus sleeps; but I go, that I may awake him out of **sleep.** Then his disciples said, Lord, if he sleeps, he will do well. [Jesus spoke of his death; but they thought that he had spoken of taking a rest in sleep].

Daniel: 12:2.

And many of them that **sleep** in the dust of the Earth **shall** awake, some to everlasting life, and some to shame…Notice it plainly states 'they shall'—(that simply means it hasn't happened yet, they are still asleep).

Psalms: 13:3.
Lighten my eyes, lest I sleep the sleep of death (KJV).

It's hard for me to understand why any church would invent something that is such an obvious lie. The only thing I can reason is that they must have believed that no–one would ever bother to read the actual text.

Chapter Seven

MURDER

As I began to write this material, I didn't plan to get involved with the attacks on the content of the Bible. However, Richard Dawkins has provided us with a fine example of what happens when someone 'scans' the text for passages that might justify a particular point–of–view. I won't cover the first part of his rant, (because we'll be here all day). I will instead correct the outright blunder he has made by describing––"The Levite and His Concubine." Then back up the point, by using text from the very next page––"The Israelites Punish the Benjaminites." (If only he had read a few more verses, before he got so excited).

This fantastic story [of his] starts at the (1:13:16) mark in the movie and runs straight into the book of Judges.

"In the Book of Judges a priest was traveling with his ex–wife in Gibea. They spent the night in the house of an old man. But, during supper, an angry mob came to demand that the man of the house 'hand over' his male guest, "So that we may know him." The old man replied, "... do not so wickedly, behold here is my daughter, and *his* concubine, them I will bring out now. [The householder knew that the mob would have killed the man, and he also knew the terrible consequences that would follow. Also, he was in a state of shock because of the sudden attack (of terror), and he simply didn't have time to think about what he was saying].

The concubine was taken by the mob then beaten and murdered by them. Neither the Bible, nor the God of the Bible murdered the woman. All the Bible writer did was record these events!

Now we should continue on to find out what God thinks about the events of that night... Try to remember the provocation for this is clearly from an enemy. We soon take up the story the following day. But first be clear that the woman had left her marriage and returned to her old life with her parents. Also be clear that **it was her parents who caused the delay.** If the man had he been allowed, he would have left early and completed the journey in a safe manner. It is also important to appreciate that the woman would have been returning as a witness. She had witnessed the decline of morality in the region, and in those days the work of two witnesses was very important, whereas the work of just one witness would not have as much potential.

The next day when the visitor saw that the woman was dead, he put her limp body across his donkey and set out for home. When he got home he took out a knife and cut her limb–by–limb into twelve parts, and sent one piece to every ruler of Israel. [This was done so that all the people could see how much she had been beaten]. Everyone who saw it was saying to one another, "Such a thing has never been seen or done, not since the Israelites came up out of Egypt. Just Imagine! We must do something! So speak up!"

Then all Israel from Dan to Beersheba and from the land of Gilead came together as one... 400,000 men––armed with swords. The tribes of Israel sent messengers throughout the tribe of Benjamin, saying "What about this awful crime that was committed among you? Now turn those wicked men of Gibea over to us so that we may put them to death and purge this evil from the tribes of Israel."

But the Benjaminites would not listen to their fellow Israelites. [Then a few paragraphs on from there we take up the story again...]

"Shall we go up again to fight against Benjamin, our fellow Israelites, or not? The Lord responded, "Go––for tomorrow I will give them into your hands."

There's much more to the story. The angry mob wouldn't kill the local family because that would bring them too much trouble. They didn't kill the Levite because that would also bring trouble from the tribes of Israel, but the woman was only a witness, killing her was the best way (in their minds) to harm the Levite and to put an end to whatever he was planning to do when he returned.

I have given you just enough of the story to show the deception used by people who cut out a few words (which seem to fit their personal views), (but without considering the whole story); A bit like any of the news services in Australia, really. That kind of news appeals to dull minded viewers but cannot be called truthful, by any measure, (at best it could be called half truthful and all sensational).

An interesting point is made, which can be applied to the present time. If the tribe of Benjamin had dealt with the criminal element in their region, there wouldn't be any need for the 400,000 angry men, ready to declare war.

Also in one of Richard Dawkins' stories the matter of 'stoning people to death' was raised. The story about stoning is linked to a well–known saying that's still around today.

This should clear up any doubt you may have about taking the law into your own hands, (or making your own judgment against another person). The old saying is… "Let he who is without sin cast the first stone."

In the following paragraphs, there's a crowd of ignorant people ready to carry out an unjust punishment.

This is a story from Luke: 8; which helps to clarify whether present day readers should be using ancient writings to justify their deeds. But before we move on, I need to make a comment about Dawkins' using a few sound bytes from the Bible, to bolster his personal views. It would be the equivalent of me taking a few passages (from a single book about Louis Pasteur) to prove a scientific point about the impossible nature of 'Abiogenesis'…(the spontaneous generation of life) it simply wouldn't have any meaning unless a full account is given, accompanied by a full explanation of the facts, <u>and the same rule applies to all</u>.

He also makes the claim that the Books are 'internally contradictory.' Yet they have the same theme throughout. Yes that's right, the same theme throughout––and all in agreement. The books of the Bible cover the lives of the Tribes of Israel, along with other peoples as they come into contact with them. Most importantly, the Books are about a future kingdom <u>here on Earth</u>, that point cannot be missed.

It's easy for people today, to sit down at the computer and research a particular subject; but that was not the case in the time these Books were written. Many towns did not have the early scrolls available, and when they did, there were only one or two copies. One copy was available for **all** to read and one to keep in a safe place. The overall theme throughout The Book is––The good news of "the future kingdom **from** heaven." Given the difficulties for past research, keeping the message of the kingdom throughout The Books is a staggering achievement.

Bible writers couldn't just turn on the computer, or drive down to the local library. Sometimes they had to walk vast distances to read a single scroll. And if someone else were ahead of them they would have to either wait, or come back another day. Another potential problem for keeping things in order was the two different languages. The New Testament scrolls were preserved in the Greek language and yet, some of the stories they would need to investigate, (if they were dumb and wanted to be deceptive), were in fact recorded in the Hebrew language. Another problem was the way the scrolls were written. It's hard to imagine trying to find a particular passage, without chapters, without numbered verses and without punctuation.

Now back to story found in John: 8.

"And early in the morning He came again into the temple, and all the people came unto Him; and He sat down, and taught them.

And the Scribes and Pharisees brought unto him a woman taken in adultery; and when they had set her in the midst, they said unto Him, 'Master, this woman was taken in adultery, in the very act. Now Moses in the law commanded us, that such should be stoned; but what do you say?' But Jesus stooped down, and with *His* finger wrote on the ground, *as though He heard them not.* So when they continued asking Him, He lifted himself up, and said unto them, **"He who is without sin among you—let him cast the first stone..."** And again he stooped down, and wrote on the ground. And they which heard *it*, being convicted, *by their own conscience*, went out one by one, beginning at the eldest *even* unto the last: and Jesus was left, and the woman standing in the midst. When Jesus had lifted himself up, and saw none but the woman, He said unto her, Woman, where are those your accusers? Haven't any of them condemned you? She said, "No man has, Lord." And Jesus said, "neither do I condemn you, go, and sin no more."

That same sentence translated directly into the Australian language would simply say: "be on your way, and stop breaking the law."

To be clear about the following paragraph, first consider that The Ten Commandments (according to that famous Book) are from God, who claims to be their Author. The command 'you shall not kill' is not an optional extra, it is a law that cannot be changed, and cannot be undermined in any way. According to the words of 'The Book' itself.

So Dawkins continues... "If you take the Good Book to its extreme (and some people do) you can justify murder."

Here he shows that it is the extremists (lurking alongside the many false religions) who give themselves the right to kill. Perhaps believing they had the same rights as the early Universal church. We see from history that after the Catholics wiped out the fourth commandment, they soon began a process of tormenting and then killing anyone who didn't follow their man-made tradition. And that I'm afraid to say, is a very real example of false religion in action.

Now back to the work of Richard Dawkins:

"In 1994, Paul Hill shot and killed Dr. John Britain outside his abortion clinic in Florida.

In 2003, Hill was executed for murder, but he went to his death *claiming* his actions were backed by holy–scripture.

I'm going to meet Paul Hill's friend and defender, Michael Bray." Dawkins: "On what moral basis could he, as a 'christian,' defend a self–professed, cold–blooded killer? You're friend Paul Hill, who was convicted of murdering a doctor, he took the law into his own hands, didn't he?"

Michael Bray: "No, Paul Hill by his own testimony acted defensively. Not in retribution, that's the job of the law, the job of the law is to punish. The job for citizens is indeed to protect one another."

A message for Paul Hill (about the law):

Luke: 6:37: Judge not, and you shall not be judged: condemn not, and you will not be condemned: forgive, and you will be forgiven. If that fellow really were a genuine priest, he would have read The Book, (and taken Luke's advice)!

This is not about whether the doctor was right or wrong, (in his actions). The question is 'does one person have the right to judge another person?' The doctor may well have been a cold–blooded killer just like Paul Hill, but that's not a reason for personal revenge. Leave the punishment to the proper authority. Murdering another person cannot be justified, not by man's laws and certainly not 'by the book.'

The same rule applies to murdering oneself (suicide); there is a message that is often used (successfully), when talking to someone who is about to do something silly; (like jump off a bridge). The jumper might say something like… "I have all these terrible problems, I can't seem to sort things out; I'm better off just ending it all now." Then a helper can quietly say to them, "what if someone, some day, figures out how to bring your body back to life. Then you may still have all your terrible problems—and a murder charge as well."

For the brief summary that follows, I would like you to slip in the word '**false**' before the word 'religion,' then the message becomes much clearer.

Dawkins: "It was curious, I quite liked him, I thought he was sincere, I thought he wasn't really an evil person. I was reminded of a quotation by the famous American physicist; 'Stephen Weinburg' (Nobel Prize winning theoretical physicist). Weinburg said; "[-----] Religion is an insult to human dignity—without it, you'd have good people doing good things, and evil people doing evil things—But for good people to do evil things, it takes [-----] religion."

WINDOWS

Dawkins: "I want to examine how science reveals the true roots of human morality. Morality stems, not from some [fictional] deity and his text, but from altruistic genes that have been 'naturally selected' in our 'evolutionary' past."

Oliver Curry: (London School of Economics)? "Humans have much more sophisticated versions of the kind of social instincts you see in chimps and other creatures—really there's no great leap; its just, if you can think of chimps as 'ms–dos' and humans as 'Windows 2000.'

Well, as I said at the start, I don't want to get into a debate over evolution, I want to stick to the overall idea of exposing false religion. But if you're a science teacher, and your using the example above, you should set the students an extra question for homework. (Since this is comparing forward progress)—What did the 'ms–dos' computer have going for it, that the chimp couldn't possibly have had?

I am sure you will find some intelligent replies.

I am finishing off this first section with a message from Ian McEwan, followed by an appropriate final statement by Richard Dawkins. And for my part, I hope that some of you have come to appreciate the coverage given by Dawkins and I hope you come to understand that religion (as it has become) must be removed from our education system.

Ian McEwan:

"I guess my starting point would be, the brain is responsible for consciousness, and we could be reasonably sure that when that brain ceases to be, when it falls apart and decomposes, that'll be the end of it. From that point a lot of things follow, I think, especially morally."

"We are the very privileged owners of a brief spark of consciousness, and we therefore have to take responsibility for it. You cannot rely on a world elsewhere—a paradise to which one can work towards, and maybe make sacrifices, and crucially make sacrifices of other people. We have a marvelous gift, and you see it develop in children—this ability to become aware that other people have minds, just like your own, and feelings that are just as important as your own. And this **gift** of empathy, seems to me to be the building block of our moral system..."

Richard Dawkins:

"Look around you, nature demands our attention, begs us to explore, to question. Religion can provide only facile, unsatisfying answers. Science, in constantly seeking real explanations, reveals the true majesty of our world, in all its complexity. People sometimes say there must be more than just this world, than just this life—but how much more do you want?"

"We are going to die, and that makes us the lucky ones. Most people are never going to die, because they're never going to be born. The number of people that could be here in my place out–number the sand grains of Sahara. If you think about all the different ways in which our genes could be permuted, you and I are quite grotesquely lucky to be here. There were a number of events that had to happen in order for you or me to exist.

We are **privileged** to be alive, and we should make the most of our time on this world."

Presented by: Professor   Richard   DawkinsUniversity   of Oxford

Chapter Nine

THE REST

"The Rest" in this case has a double meaning. On the one hand, this chapter is the beginning of the rest of the book. It is also a story about "The Rest."

What on Earth could possibly drive someone, anyone, to take on a desire to remove the first day of the week, and then shove it all the way down into eighth place, and then push all seven days back one place, deceptively re-engineering the working week? Well that is exactly what happened when someone decided to make a different calendar. The new week would supposedly make it easier to force people to "remember" a false 'seventh day.'

When you think about it, making a different week on the calendar would be simpler than recalling all the Books and then 'attacking them with a marking pen.'

But something serious had to be done in order to set-up and then maintain a new 'traditional belief.' The inventor of the new week would have been bitterly disappointed, when he realised that his efforts were in vain.

Although some Australians are content to call Sunday a part of the "weekend," there is no doubt, that Sunday is the first working day of the week––by definition.

SUN"DAY, n. {'christian' sabbath}; the first day of the week.
[Webster's Revised Unabridged Dictionary (1828)]

This chapter explains a little, about––Sunday versus Sabbath––(technically sundown Friday to sundown Saturday). The Sunday problem also gets a mention in the 'Ishtar' chapter.

Firstly, how the Roman leaders supposedly gave themselves the "authority" to change over to Sunday, (to invent their own tradition). Their **supposed** authority comes from the book of Matthew:

"And I say also unto you, that you are Peter; and upon **this** **Rock**; I will build my church; and nothing shall prevail against it. And I will give unto you the keys of the kingdom from Heaven: and whatsoever you shall bind on Earth shall be bound in Heaven: and whatsoever you shall loose on Earth shall be loosed in Heaven." [Matthew: 16:18]

It's easy to see how someone could become confused by those verses, however the leaders at the time, would have been reading this in another language, the true meaning (then) would have been much clearer. The deception applied to these verses was no accident! By referring to the Greek definition, the difference between two 'rocks' is obvious.

The word translated 'Peter', is from the Greek word 'petros' apparently a primary word; a piece of rock. So you can see that the name 'Peter' means 'a piece of rock' (a little bigger than a small stone). That's exactly how it would have read to them—all those years ago. The second 'Rock' is translated from the word 'Petra.' meaning a mass of rock (literally or figuratively): Rock. So we end up with a translation that makes sense—"You are Peter," (followed by referring to Himself). "And upon **This Rock** I will build my church."

It only 'appears' that some part of The Book gives 'authority' to Peter and a new church (to change whatever they like). Common–sense tells us that even if any church were allowed to bind anything, or loose anything, it would have to be within the boundaries of the recorded laws, and as in the sentence, it would be AFTER the kingdom from Heaven has arrived here on Earth. So He could only be referring to a future time. It's fair to say, (at the time of writing this book), The Lord has not returned or His kingdom. (The actual city will arrive approx 1100 years later). (When you get to the part describing 'that great city' you are nearly at the end of Revelation). Please note: the text says 'I will' (future). And I will give unto you the keys of the kingdom [from] heaven: and whatsoever you shall bind on Earth... and so–on. Notice that it is written clearly "I will"(future). Notice also that the words 'of heaven' are clear. This is definitely not referring to Peter being shot off to heaven. Peter may someday be given the right to 'enter' The Kingdom, but such an event must occur after The Great City lands on Earth [from] 'Heaven' and whatever Peter does after that must be aligned with the laws of God.

He most certainly was not given authority at the time referred to, in the book of Matthew. If you doubt it, simply skip forward to verse 23: (...He turned, and said unto Peter, 'Get behind me Satan: you are an offence to me: for you savour not the things of God, but those that be of men'). So the more you look into it, the more you realise that the supposed authority, of a "man–made church" was never more than an elaborate hoax. The man (Peter) was only human after all, just a regular person like you or me.

Some will complain that the present seventh day cannot be the same because some days were taken out of the month in the year 1582 (to make an adjustment). Actually only the 'dates' were changed; Thursday, October 4th, was followed by Friday, October 15th. Now let's see what the 'Sunday keepers' have to say about Sunday, by reading through some of their own material...

"I have repeatedly offered one thousand dollars to anyone who can prove to me, (by the Bible alone), that I am bound to keep Sunday. There is no such law in the Bible. It is a law of the [holy] Catholic Church alone. The Bible says 'Remember that you keep holy the Sabbath day. The Catholic Church says, No! By my 'divine' power I abolish the Sabbath day, and command you to keep holy the first day of the week. And lo! The entire civilized world bows down in reverent obedience to the command of the [holy] Catholic Church."

[Bishop Thomas Enright, in a personal letter, printed in 'Experiences of a Pioneer Minister of Minnesota' W.B. Hill]

And from Peter Geiermann;
"Question: which day is the Sabbath day?
Answer: Saturday is the Sabbath day.
Question: Why do we observe Sunday instead of Saturday?
Answer: We observe Sunday instead of Saturday because the Catholic Church in the council of Laodicea (AD 363), transferred the solemnity to Sunday." ['The Convert's Catechism of Catholic Doctrine.']

And from a story of A Catholic telling the other Sunday-keepers to go back to the God of The Bible).

Protestants, who accept the Bible as the only rule of faith and religion, should by all means go back to the observance of the Sabbath. The fact that they do not, but on the contrary observe Sunday, stultifies them in the eyes of every thinking man.

We Catholics do not accept the Bible as the only rule of faith. Besides the Bible we have the living church, the authority of the Church to guide us. We say, this church, to teach and guide man through life, has the right to change the ceremonial laws of the Old Testament and thence we accept her change of the Sabbath to Sunday. We frankly say, yes, the Church made this change, made this law, as she made many other laws, for instance the Friday abstinence, the unmarried priesthood, the laws concerning mixed marriages, the regulation of Catholic marriages, **and a thousand other laws**...It is always somewhat laughable to see the Protestant churches, in pulpit and legislation, demand the observance of Sunday, **of which there's nothing in their Bible.**

Anyone can see from these quotes (and hundreds of others) that The Catholic Church wants the exclusive right to Sunday. They want the daughter churches to give up on Sunday and return to God and keep the Sabbath as commanded in the holy Bible.

And if they did turn back to The God of the Bible, they would soon find out just how important the seventh day is…

Have you ever heard the old saying, 'Manna from Heaven?' The casual reader would not expect to find 'manna' in a story about 'The Rest,' however such a story shows the true importance of the seventh–day.

Hebrew: **Manna**; literally, a what–ness (so to speak), i.e. manna (so called from the question about it) **"What is it?"**
(Because such a thing had never been seen).

O"mer (?), n. [Cf. Homer.] A Hebrew measure, the tenth of an ephah.
[Webster's Revised Unabridged Dictionary (1913)]
(Aren't you glad I cleared that up)?

Exodus: 16:13
In the morning the dew lay round about the host. And when the dew that lay was gone up, behold, upon the face of the wilderness there lay a small round thing, as small as the white frost on the ground. And when the children of Israel saw it, they said one to another, It is manna: for they wist not what it was. And Moses said unto them. "This is the bread which the Lord has given you to eat. This is the thing which the Lord has commanded, gather of it every man according to his eating, an omer for everyone, according to the number of your persons; take you every man, for them which are in his tents." And the children of Israel did so, and gathered; some more; some less. And when they did mete it out with an omer, he that gathered much had nothing over, and he that gathered little had no lack; they gathered every man according to his eating. And Moses said, Let no man leave of it till the morning.

Notwithstanding they hearkened not unto Moses; but some of them left of it until the morning, and it bred worms, and stank:

and Moses was wroth with them. And they gathered it every morning, every man according to his eating: and when the sun waxed hot, it melted. And it came to pass, that on the sixth day they gathered twice as much, two omers for one man: and all the rulers of the congregation came and told Moses. And he said unto them; Tomorrow is The Rest of the holy Sabbath unto The Lord: Bake that which you will bake today, and seethe that you will seethe; and that which remains, lay up for you to be kept until morning.

So that on the sixth day the citizens of 'The Tribes of Israel' would set aside enough for the seventh also; (so they didn't need to 'gather' on the Sabbath). On any other day of the week the 'what-is-it' would not keep until the following day! In this way the Israelites learned the importance of **remembering and keeping the fourth commandment.**

It's fair to say, that in the past, people accepted the commandments of God much more readily than they do in the present age.

A queer thing has come from the supposed 'authority' of Peter. In this present era, strange talk about floating off to heaven can lead to jokes about 'dead–people' seeing St. Peter at "The Pearly Gates."

The actual text of the Book is quite different from this popular man-made idea. The following is an advance account, a 'virtual reality' experience that John was inspired to record in the first century A.D.

Revelation 21:2:

And I John saw the Holy City, coming **down** from God out of heaven...(KJV)

Revelation 21:10:
And he carried me away in the spirit to a great and high mountain, and showed me that great city, **descending** out of 'heaven'...(KJV)

Revelation 21:21:

47

And the twelve gates were twelve pearls; every gate was of one pearl: and the street of the city was pure gold, as if it were transparent glass (KJV).

John's message to the church and the citizens is very plain. If Peter is ever going to see the 'pearl gates' it will be here on Earth (after the city has descended from 'heaven').

You may have noticed in an earlier chapter the great universal church has decreed that their followers should 'talk to Mary' which, of course is an utterly absurd thing to do. In this, you see the opposite condition––instead of being told to do something absurd––the followers are forced to neglect something that is vital, that is––The Fourth Commandment.

Now take the time to consider each of the 'Ten Commandments,' and to consider, if it is necessary to obey. Or have they been 'done away with.'

First take another look at some of the things the churches believe and teach, in order to answer this question, 'Are they reading and obeying an Instruction Book? Or are they living in a fantasy world of their own invention?'

Ask yourself these questions...

Does The Book support "A tree–ceremony"—NO!

Does it support "Praying to a dead Mary"— NO!

Does it support "Floating off into heaven"— NO!

Does it support "A bad–time in hell"— NO!

Does it support "Halloween"— NO!

Does it support "Easter"— NO!

Does it support "Good–friday"— NO!

Does it support "Sunday services"— NO!

Does it support "a 'triune' or 'trinity'"— NO!

Does it support "a young–Earth"— NO!

The most popular teaching of our time is that the commandments of God have been done-away with. All you have to do; they say; is just believe in God and you will be saved. But, is that what God says?

Definitely not. In fact even our human definition shows that being saved is directly linked to the avoidance of sin. So to completely discuss the fourth commandment we need to discover if it is still IN The Bible, and we need to determine if it should be obeyed to this day, or is it simply to be ignored, as taught by the Sunday churches and their various offshoots.

From the New Testament.
1 John 5:3:
For this is the love of God,
that we keep his commandments:
and his commandments are not grievous.
In the following passages there are 'pairs.'

The first of each, is the true record from The Book;
the second; [enclosed]; is the "adjusted" version—
(peddled as the truth).

One: I am the LORD your God, which has brought you out of the land of Egypt, out of the house of bondage. You shall have no other gods before me.

Later altered to read…(one)

[I am the Lord your God: you shall not have strange gods before me].

Two: You shall not make unto you any graven image, or any likeness of any thing that is in heaven above, or that is in the earth beneath, or that is in the water under the earth: You shall not bow down to them, nor serve them: for I the Lord your God am a jealous God, visiting the iniquity of the fathers upon the children unto the third and fourth generation of them that hate me; And showing mercy unto thousands of them that love me, **and keep my commandments**.

Later altered to read…(two)
[You shall not take the name of the Lord in vain].

Three: You shall not take the name of the LORD your God in vain; for the LORD will not hold him guiltless that takes his name in vain.

Later altered to read…(three)
[Remember that you keep holy the sabbath day].

Four: Remember the Sabbath Day, to keep **it** holy. Six days shall you labour, and do all your work: But the **seventh** day is the sabbath of the Lord your God: in it you shall not do any work, you, nor your son, nor your daughter, your manservant, nor your maidservant, nor your cattle, nor a stranger that is within your gates: For in six days the Lord 'made' heaven and earth, the sea, and all that in them is, and rested the seventh day: wherefore the Lord blessed the sabbath day, and hallowed it.

Altered to read…(four)
[Honour your father and your mother].

Five: Honour your father and your mother: that your days may be long upon the land which the Lord your God giveth thee.
Altered to read...(five)
[Thou shalt not kill].

Six: Thou shalt not kill.

Altered to read...(six)
[Thou shalt not commit adultery].

Seven: Thou shalt not commit adultery.
Altered to read...(seven)
[Thou shalt not steal]

Eight: Thou shalt not steal.
Altered to read...(eight)
[Thou shalt not bear false witness aginst a neighbour].

Nine: You shall not bear false witness against your neighbour.
Altered to read...(nine)
[You shall not covet your neighbour's wife].

Ten: You shall not covet your neighbour's house, you shall not covet your neighbour's wife, nor his manservant, nor his maidservant, nor his ox, nor his ass, nor any thing that is your neighbour's.

Altered to read...(ten)
[You shall not covet thy neighbour's goods].

The first of each shown comes from the Instruction Book and will never change.

The second; [below each one] is taken from ...
[the Convert's Catechism of Catholic doctrine. P 37; published by B. Herder Book Co. (1921)]

These rediculous changes were made, almost in the same fashion as shuffling the days of the week. Just move them up one place and hope that no one notices the deception. If you keep away from what the catholic church has done and keep away from their mindless followers, (the other Sun-day churches), then I can assure you that the fourth command is still in place, as it always has been. Now we need to consider if these commands are of any importance to you.

To enable you to consider if in fact the commands are relevant today I offer the following quotes so you can let "The Book" show for itself if the above-mentioned changes are truly lawful [or just plain awful].

Matthew 5:18

For verily I say unto you, *Till heaven and earth pass, one jot or one tittle shall in no wise pass from the law*, (KJV)

Matthew 15:9
But in vain do they worship me, teaching for doctrines the commandments of men.

Matthew 19:17
And he said unto him, Why callest me good? there is none good but one, that is God: but if you will enter into life, **keep the commandments**.

Mark 7:7
Howbeit in vain do they worship me, teaching for doctrines the commandments of men.

Luke 1:6
And they were both righteous before God, walking in **all the commandments** and ordinances of the Lord.

John 14:15

If you love me, **keep my commandments.**

Any reasonable person must be able to see that the Ten Commandments of God are not done away with. If you choose to believe in an all powerful Being then you should accept Him as the author of the Bible. Wherever His book remains unaltered it means exactly what it says. The rules and laws have not changed in any way, and the good news of the coming kingdom of God is consistent throughout the book, and has never changed.

Chapter Ten

EPHRAIM AND MANASSEH

Ephraim and Manasseh are the names of two of the twelve tribes of Israel. The descendants of Ephraim are mostly located in England, Australia, New Zealand and Canada. The descendants of Manasseh are generally found in The United States of America.

Throughout The Book there is a great deal of information about two brothers: Jacob and Esau. Stepping back from there (a little); we can find the story of Abraham's son; Isaac; and Isaac's wife Rebekah: they were trying to have a child; (a son to carry on the inheritance). This was a period when having a son was important, (and a first son would receive a greater portion).

Come back to these definitions or quotes if needed! This partly describes where the twelve tribes originated. –

But first, please consider the definition of the words Jacob and Esau; from the Hebrew language; also the definition of...

Bowels: [me`ah may-aw'] from an unused root, meaning to be soft; used only in plural: the intestines, or (collectively) the abdomen, figuratively, sympathy; by implication, a vest; by extension, the stomach, the uterus, the heart (figuratively): belly; **or womb.**

Jacob: [Ya`aqob] {yah-ak-obe'} (i.e. supplanter); Jaakob, patriarch; from `aqab aw-kab' a primitive root; properly, to swell out or up; to seize by the heel; figuratively, to circumvent (as if tripping up the heels); also to restrain (as if holding by the heel): take by the heel, stay, supplant-utterly.

Esau: 'Esav ay-sawv' apparently a form of the passive participle of 'asah aw-saw' in the original sense of handling rough (i.e. sensibly felt); the Israelitish Esav, a son of Isaac, including his posterity.

Genesis 25:21: And Isaac intreated the LORD for his wife, because she was barren: and the LORD was intreated of him, and Rebekah his wife conceived. And the children struggled together within her; and she said, "If it be so, why am I thus?" And she went to enquire of the LORD. And the LORD said unto her. "Two nations are in thy womb, and two manner of people shall be separated from thy bowels; and the one people shall be stronger than the other people; and the elder shall serve the younger (KJV)."

Genesis 25:24: And when her days to be delivered were fulfilled, behold, there were twins in her womb. And the first came out red all over, like a hairy garment; and they called his name Esau. And after that came his brother out, and his hand took hold on Esau's heel; and his name was called Jacob: and Isaac was threescore years old when *she* bare them. And the boys grew: and Esau was a cunning hunter, a man of the field; and Jacob was a plain man, dwelling in tents.

Genesis 27:36: And he said, "Is not he rightly named Jacob? For he has supplanted me these two times: he took away my birthright; and, behold now he has taken away my blessing. And he said, "Have you not reserved a blessing for me?"

Genesis 32:28; And He said, "Your name shall be called no more Jacob, but Israel: for as a prince have you power with God and with men, and have prevailed."

Israel had twelve sons—Reuben, Simeon, Levi, Judah, Zebulon, Issachar, Dan, Gad, Asher, Naphtali, Joseph and Benjamin. These families grew into a nation.

Israel lived in Egypt, in the country of Goshen; and they had possessions, and multiplied.

Numbers 2:1: And the LORD spoke unto Moses and unto Aaron, saying, every man of the children of Israel shall pitch by his own standard, with the ensign of their father's house: around the 'Tent of Meeting' at a distance. (KJV)

Numbers 13:11: And the Lord spoke unto Moses, saying, Send your men, that they may search the land of Canaan, which I give unto the children of Israel: of every tribe of their fathers shall you send a man, every one a ruler among them. And Moses by the commandment of the Lord sent them from the wilderness of Paran: All those men were heads of the children of Israel, and these were their names:

Of the tribe of Reuben,
Shammua the son of Zaccur.

Of the tribe of Simeon,
Shaphat the son of Hori.

Of the tribe of Judah,
Caleb the son of Jephunneh.

Of the tribe of Issachar,
Igal the son of Joseph.

Of the tribe of Ephraim,
Oshea the son of Nun.

Of the tribe of Benjamin,
Palti the son of Raphu.

Of the tribe of Zebulun,
Gaddiel the son of Sodi.

Of the tribe of Joseph,
(namely) of the tribe of Manasseh,

Gaddi the son of Susi.

Of the tribe of Dan,
Ammiel the son of Gemalli.

Of the tribe of Asher,
Sethur the son of Michael.

Of the tribe of Naphtali,
Nahbi the son of Vophsi.

Of the tribe of Gad,
Geuel the son of Machi.

These are the names of the men; which Moses sent to spy out the land. And Moses called Oshea, Jehoshua.

Notice that in the list of sons of Israel there are Levi and Joseph, but in the list of men that were sent out, Levi isn't there. Ephraim and Manasseh are now on the list. This happened because 'The Tribe of Levi,' by now, would have been 'set aside,' to be the priests for 'The Tent of Meeting.' Ephraim and Manesseh were both of The Tribe of Joseph. Their camp eventually became well–organised; each tribe set–up around The Tent of Meeting, according to their family name.

To the north:	Nepthali,	Asher,	Dan.
To the south:	Rueben,	Simeon,	Gad.
To the east:	Zebulan,	Issachar,	Judah.
To the west:	Ephraim,	Manasseh,	Benjamin.

And the tribe of Dan would move away from Israel (and seem to have lost their right to be included in the twelve, along the way). Dan traveled in ships and ended up settling in Ireland; (after leaving a trail of places with their father's name). Even though the tribe of

Dan took–off at the wrong time, they may have paved the way for later migrations to other countries (like Scotland and England).

Now I am going way off the timeline here, but it is important to note that in Revelation 'The Tribe of Dan is missing from the list and The Tribe of Levi is included; also note that Manasseh and Joseph are there. On the latter list 'Ephraim' is shown as 'The Tribe of Joseph.'

If you're living in Australia *and* you prefer your week starting with Sunday; you could be related to Ephraim.

Firms operating in Australia will sometimes issue a non-Australian (Mon–Sun) 'promotional calendar' thinking they are getting some sort of 'advertising,' year–round; However most people I know will toss out that calendar, unless it's an Australian version (Sunday to Saturday). Sometimes it's a tad hard to believe that Ephraim and Manasseh are closely related; as well as a different working week consider the different words and spelling of words. In Australia we put petrol in the car, luggage in the boot and then head off down the left hand side of the road. Americans put gas in the car, luggage in the trunk, and head off down the right hand side of the road.

There's also different spelling in words like colour and labour and so on. And when I type a word like organization; this spell checker automatically changes the 's' to a 'z,' and so on…

There is often a certain hidden 'style' in a company, disclosed by their name or title. There are many businesses in Australia that have an Australian sounding name, yet they are American through and through. One sure giveaway is the type of calendar they produce.

[A brand–name for you to consider carefully is "The Australian Labor Party." Such a name is a contradiction! To give it the full and rightful title it would be "The American Labor Party in Australia."

If the Labor Party had its roots in Ephraim it would be named The Australian 'Labour' Party, with a 'u', just as it is in Britain (and should be in Australia). This 'Labor' party in Australia wants to change our country to a republic, but Australians are not ready for such a change. Our women are not ready to be called madam and our men are not ready to be called sir. From what I can see, the majority of Australians do not have a problem with royalty.

The hardened Labor supporters are the main offenders when it comes to making a mockery of our English heritage. It was a great shame (in 2015) to see the 'Labor' party making a mockery of the English system, just before Prince Harry came to Australia for a visit; A type of (Republicanism by Stealth), and it was totally inappropriate (at the time).

Some of the descendents; of the tribes–of–Israel are;

The tribe of **Manasseh** is basically the **United States.**

The tribe of **Ephraim** is mainly the English-speaking countries of the British Commonwealth. (Canada, New Zealand, parts of South Africa and **Australia**).

The modern-day Jews (scattered among the nations) are known to be of the tribe of Judah, A large portion of them live in a place named Israel. The following article briefly shows the 'organisation' of the Twelve Tribes.

The children of Israel fled Egypt in haste. They possessed no means of settling disputes, maintaining 'law and order,' or chain of command. However the time in the wilderness was used to establish and organize them.

The Tribe of Reuben:

The tribe of Reuben descended from the firstborn son of Jacob and Leah. As the firstborn son, Reuben played a prominent role in the early accounts. However, his role as a tribe would diminish significantly over time.

The Tribe of Simeon:

The tribe of Simeon was descended from the second born son of Jacob and Leah. This tribe dwelt in relative obscurity, and had very little impact on the history of Israel.

The Tribe of Levi:

The tribe of Levi was descended from the third son of Jacob and Leah. Through an act of faithfulness in the wilderness, this tribe would become 'set apart' by God.

The Tribe of Judah:

The tribe of Judah became one of the most prominent tribes in all of Israel. The Davidic Dynasty emerged from this tribe, a lineage that culminated in the birth of Jesus.

The Tribe of Dan:

The tribe of Dan is perhaps the most enigmatic of the twelve. Their downfall may be linked to the captured idol (Molech). They failed to drive out their Philistine and Canaanite neighbours. As a result, they migrated to another land, in the northernmost limits of Canaan.

The Tribe of Naphtali:

Naphtali was the sixth son of Jacob, and the second produced by Bilhah. Naphtali was blessed by Jacob, on his deathbed. The tribe of Naphtali was a tribe of great warriors, and took part in some of the most important battles.

The Tribe of Gad:

Gad was the seventh son of Jacob and Zilpah, (Leah's maiden). Gad became the Marines. They were fierce, athletic, and skillful on the battlefield. They played lead roles in the conquest of Sihon and Og and led the Israelites across the Jordan to Jericho.

The Tribe of Asher:

The tribe of Asher proved to be a tribe of contradictions and vagaries. Influenced by the pagan religion of Phoenicia and chastised by Deborah, the tribe also came to the aid of Gideon, and supplied king David with one-third of his army (in Hebron).

The Tribe of Issachar:

The tribe of Issachar earned a reputation as students of the law. They were wise men, well respected. Scripture calls them princes. However, the infamous King Baasha and son were descended from this tribe.

The Tribe of Zebulun:

The tenth son of Jacob would prove to be faithful. The tribe fought bravely with Deborah and Barak. They were mentioned in conjunction with Gideon. The tribe took part in an important prophecy of Isaiah's.

The Tribe of Ephraim:

Perhaps no tribe symbolises man's struggle with God more than the tribe of Ephraim.
At once rebuked, then praised, Ephraim was always under the watchful eye of God. The name would come to represent the entire northern kingdom. The Ephraimites participated in many of Israel's engagements throughout the period known as Judges.

The Tribe of Benjamin:

Of the 12 tribes, Benjamin is one of only two, to appear throughout the entire Bible. They are the only tribe to have belonged to both the north and the south. The tribe of Benjamin played an integral part in many events from Judges through to Ezra. Benjaminites such as king Saul and the great prophet Samuel significantly shaped history. Queen Esther was a descendant of the tribe of Benjamin. The Tribe of Benjamin, thus, produced not only a king, but also a queen. Esther would rise to become Queen of Persia.

The Tribe of Manasseh:

The Tribe of Manasseh was the only one to inherit land on both sides of the Jordan River. This was because of the double-portion given to Manasseh, the eldest of Joseph.

The following is a brief description of the story from Judges where the men of The Tribe of Dan seize a **false priest** and his carved image. (A piece of wood cut from the forest and decked with silver and with gold).

The Tribe of Dan had little concern for the laws of God, or the law of the land, (they went their own way).

[And the five men that went to spy out the land went into Micah's house, and fetched the carved image. Then the priest asked, "What are you doing?"

And they said to him, "Hold your peace, lay your hand on your mouth, and go with us,"]

It's the beginning of the end for Dan. They no longer needed The God of the Bible. They had their false artifact and a false priest to go with it!

Chapter Eleven

'SANDY CLAWS'

As Richard has suggested, future generations might learn to investigate the origin of "ancient and mysterious ways," *before* they become infected. Such free spirits should be able to break free from the vice of religion altogether.

Such an effort would end the process of passing on the false— from generation to generation. This chapter takes a look at a very popular but unsavoury character; (who hangs around shopping malls in our country). Some of this takes a look at where he originated from; and whether he belongs on your list of 'things–to–do.'

To make the task simpler; please take another look at the Instruction Book. I have already exposed the "tree" (in chapter one). Now for further proof of deception; take a look at 'Revelation;' but first we need to be sure about who or what we are looking for….

[Who are the "Nicolaitans"]?

A mysterious group of wicked **religious imposters**; were the "Nicolaitans." What did they teach? Do they still exist today? Why should they concern you? In the warnings to the seven churches of

Revelation, we are told to beware of them. Why are they dangerous and how would you recognise them?...

In Revelation, chapter 2, we read of a sect or group; called the Nicolaitans; who pose a great threat to The Church of God.

The author of The Bible says to the Ephesus church: "But this you have, that you hate the deeds of the Nicoaitans, which I also hate" (Rev.2:6)].

Always remember that the church hated and rejected the doctrines, (the practices), of the Nicolaitans.

Now that we have the background, we can easily work out where this imposter comes from.

Sandy Claws is of course "Old Saint Nicolas;" of the "Nicolaitans", also known as *"Old Saint Nick."* (Which is also a name for the devil).

The name Saint Nicolas later developed toward [saint–nee–clause] and then [saintee–clause]. The most popular rendition of it (in our time) is [santa–clause]. We were all brought up with this 'false–christian idea.'

In the present age, we do not need to pass on this distorted custom. If you would like to find out more about the tree; I suggest doing some research into ancient 'Asherim' objects. I cannot include the details of the Asherim or Ashera Pole objects, or this book might end up with an 'R' rating. It was the research of the tree–ceremony that led me to cease the 'practices of the Nicolaitans.' If the study of the ancient ceremonies isn't enough to stop you, then nothing will.

I feel at this stage that I haven't quite got the message across about the strong connection from ancient and mysterious false religions to the present day 'Sandy Claws.' In trying to cover it fully I will inevitably be going–over the same material again. I'm not trying to jam you with an idea. I am simply trying to set out some 'dots' for you to follow. You are still free to choose. Of course if you are a hardened athiest–scientist, then nothing I could say would make any difference. To the scientist, holy days are very simple to deal with. If the Catholics or any church are doing the ancient rituals then they are **medieval rituals** of faith.

On the other hand, if the scientist is taking part in a ceremony of Xmas or Ishtah they are simply harmless family tradition. I doubt that any scientist could change his mind on that.

But what about a person who belongs to the man–kind, this work is for you, you are free to think for yourself. Simply follow the 'dots' that I have laid out and then do some research. You will be able to accept the views that I am presenting, or dismiss them, entirely.

Some of your Xmas customs are a hand–me–down from the Druids, (Celtic priests). They arrived via The Druid priests to The Tribe of Dan and on to the modern Druids. The Druids were lovers of trees, there were dozens of different trees that they found to be important or essential in their ceremonies or rituals. The ones you should be concerned about are covered in this section…

The ancient Celts believed trees to be very important. Trees were used for fuel and heat, as well as for cooking, building and weaponry. They believed that many of the products from trees provided a powerful 'spirit' presence. The use of trees varied between different cultures and regions. Some were thought to be "special" to many cultures. Tall trees, or trees that produced a wide range of products, trees that were unique, or perhaps trees with a 'spirit presence.' Trees become a big part of their folklore, mythology and worship.

These are some of the trees that were so important (even vital), to their weird and unlawful practices.

ALDER	APPLE (Domestic)	ASH	BIRCH	
BROOM	CEDAR	ELDER	ELM	FIR
HOLLY	MISTLETOE	OAK	PINE	
ROWAN	WILLOW	and	YEW	

The Celts had their own 'CULT of Trees,' they also 'adopted' other local cults. The Fagus Deus (the divine beech), the sex–arbors of Pyrenean inscriptions, and an anonymous god represented by a conifer on an altar at Toulouse, probably point to local Ligurian tree cults––continued on by the Celts well into Roman times. Forests were also personified or ruled by a single goddess, like 'Dea Arduinna' of the Ardennes and 'Dea Abnoba' of the Black Forest. But more primitive ideas were around, like assigning a whole class of tree-divinities to a single forest, The 'Fatæ Dervones,' spirits of the oak–woods of Northern Italy. Groups of trees like sex–arbores were venerated, perhaps for their height, isolation, or some other queer feature.

The Celts made their sacred places in dark groves, the trees being hung with offerings (or with the heads of victims). Human sacrifices were hung or impaled on trees, as practiced by the warriors of 'Boudicca.' These, like the offerings still placed, by certain people (on sacred trees), were attached (because the trees were the abode of spirits or divinities) which in many cases had power over vegetation?

Pliny said of the Celts: "They esteem nothing more sacred than the mistletoe and the tree on which it grows. But apart from this they choose oak–woods for their sacred groves, and perform no sacred rite without using oak branches." 'Maximus of Tyre' speaks of the image of Zeus as a lofty oak, and an old Irish glossary gives Daur (oak), as an early Irish name for god. The sacred "need–fire" may have been obtained by friction from oak-wood, and it is because of the 'nature' of the oak that a piece of its wood is still used as a talisman.

You should be able to notice that many of the 'special' trees from the Druid/Irish/Druid cultures are well and truly embedded in the present day customs for Sandy Claws. The book of Judges contains the story of how the Tribe of Dan obtained their priest and a 'piece of tree' – (decked with silver and with gold). You will discover that the Tribe of Dan is no longer counted with the twelve tribes of Israel. You will discover that the area where the priest and his artifact were 'captured' was near the place where the horrible attack occurred (The one in the story of the Levite). You will also find that the Tribe of Benjamin were the ones protecting the criminals. You will also discover that the tribe of Benjamin was almost completely wiped out in the war that followed.

There is little doubt that there was once a city of Dan within the Israelite nations...

An American naval officer William F. Lynch identified Tell el Kadi as the site of ancient Dan (1849). Three years later, Edward Robinson also made the same identification. His identification is now accepted as factual.

The Hebrew Bible states that the site prior to its conquest by the Tribe of Dan was known as Laysha (with slightly different spelling) within Judges, Joshua and Isaiah. The present day Judah use the name 'Tel Dan' for this site. The Tribe of Dan moved on, because they became impatient and decided to go–it–alone. Dan travelled in ships, leaving landmarks (with 'Dan' sounding names) as they make their long journey, eventually settling in Ireland. The Xmas traditions of our time are not something to be taken lightly they are an ancient religion. The Xmas traditions should never be counted as simply a harmless family gathering.

The second most popular festival (in The US) is the Halloween nonsense.

In fact, during the re–editing of my first book (in preparation for this one) the horrible virus of Halloween has spread like wildfire across [our] entire continent. This virus––which Australia had been free of for generations––is now even being taught to innocent children of pre-school age.

In America, citizens spend over two billion dollars each year on this rediculous and annoying behaviour. Besides teaching children that it's alright to beg for something—rather than working to earn it—it is also turning them into extorsionists, demanding something–for–nothing; (or I will play a nasty trick on you).

The early Encyclopaedia Britannica says the following:

["Samhain (Celtic: 'End of Summer'), one of the most important and sinister calendar festivals of the Celtic year. At Samhain, held on November 1, the world of the gods was believed to be made visible to mankind, and the gods played many tricks on their mortal worshippers; it was a time fraught with danger, charged with fear, and full of "supernatural" episodes. **Sacrifices** and propitiations of every kind were thought to be vital, for without them the Celts believed they could not prevail over the perils of the season or counteract the activities of the deities. Samhain was an important precursor to Halloween."]

Hebrew: 2:14; ...that through death he might destroy him that had the power of death, that is, the devil. (KJV)

The ancient Celts, (who actually believed they were worshipping the true God), were deceived into worshipping 'the god of this world'.

The present ruler over the Earth; is in fact "the father of lies and religious deception." The Celts also bring us the Celtic cross which many "believers" hang on their wall, falsely thinking of it as a "religious" object. You don't need an image of a helpless baby, or an image of a man, or an instrument of death. No statues, no engraved images, no images, FULL STOP. If you want to form a mental image, it would be as described by Daniel. "His face as bright as the appearance of lightning, and His eyes as lamps of fire, and His arms and His feet like the colour of polished brass, and the voice of His words like the voice of a multitude." The false religions present a weak baby or a man hanging on a tree to deny His present day appearance. The Bible claims that He shines so bright that a 3D person would be blinded at the sight of him, (when shining in full strength)!

Of all the wrong things that the Celts did, the sacrifice of innocent children was the most bizarre, yet it was an important part of their strange and unlawful practices.

Either cut out this Xmas and Halloween nonsense or teach your children the truth about human sacrifice and let *them* decide. In ancient times human sacrifice was used to sure-up those who were ill or injured. At first, criminals were chosen for sacrifice, but if there were not enough, then parents would "volunteer" their own little kids.

Giant wicker baskets were prepared and then stacked with poles and people – ready for the fire. Loud drums were played so the parents wouldn't hear the screams of their little kids as they were burned alive (in company with criminals); As the giant wicker basket was lowered into a roaring fire. The Celts genuinely believed that the death of the little kids would bring back the strength of their fighting men who had been injured in battle.

And what would God think of such a thing?

Jeremiah 32:34

(At a time when Israel and Judah have turned their backs on Gods laws...)

"But they set their abominations in the house, which is called by my name, to defile it. And they built the high places of Baal, which are in the valley of the son of Hinnom, to cause their sons and their daughters to pass through the fire unto Molech; which I commanded them not, neither came it into my mind, that they should do this abomination..."

The simple law of having no other gods would be enough for the average person to stop the annual celebration for Molech. Plus, the Bible says that it never entered 'His mind,' that human beings would celebrate the ritual of burning little kids, "to pass through the fire unto Molech." (In *your* Xmas ritual Molech is represented by 'Sandy Claws')

The murder of little kids is not a pleasant thing to be teaching your children about, (at any time). And what will you say to them if they discover the truth as they grow up?

Chapter Twelve

'Ishtar'

[Thankfully; in Australia the Halloween bug is only at the worm stage].

Yes that first sentence is exactly as I wrote it, in the draft edition of this book (just a few years ago), however that sentence is now out of date, almost all school students in Australia have been infected, helped along by arrogant and ignorant teachers and parents. And recently I have heard of this outrageous thing being shown even to preschool children. The disturbing virus of Halloween has spread further and faster than I could ever have anticipated.

Along with the rediculous Halloween, there is another favourite [here], the celebration for 'Ishtar.' This is by far the easiest hoax to investigate and expose. It comes from ancient and myterious times. A time when the 'gods' had more than one name; (the names gradually changed over time—just like Sandy Claws).

Ishtar (pronounced easter) is another name for Ashteroth.

The goddess Ishtar "the light–bringer," also known as 'the queen of heaven,' is the Babylonian high mother-goddess; the goddess of fertility, love and war.

1 Samuel: 7:3; And Samuel spake unto all the house of Israel, saying, If you do return unto the Lord with all your hearts, then put away the strange gods and Ashtaroth from among you, and prepare your hearts unto the Lord, and serve Him only: and He will deliver you out of the hand of the Philistines.

Then the children of Israel **did put away Baalim and Ashtaroth**, and served the Lord only. (KJV)
(For a while at least)

Another alias would be Astarte. According to scholar Mark S. Smith, Astarte may be the Iron Age incarnation of the Bronze Age Asherah. Astarte is the name of a goddess known from Northwestern Semitic regions, with similar, origin and functions to the goddess Ishtar (in Mesopotamian texts).

As you can see from the above; the seemingly harmless celebration; known as easter; has a dark side to it. The **eggs** are obviously symbols of **fertility**, and we all know what the **rabbits** represent. When you buy gifts for the 'queen of heaven'—you are in fact introducing a celebration of fertility. The only thing that hasn't been resolved; is whether your 'gifts' are for her 'fertility'; or otherwise.

Now that I have put your 'Ishtar Eggs' into the correct basket; you might like to consider the remainder of the deception. The whole "Good Friday—Easter Sunday tradition" is a complete fabrication. The (churches) of this world rely on...

Confusion,   Disagreement and   Competition

Yes, they rely on these to keep the Easter dream alive, but the text of the Instruction Book teaches us to recognise these 'conditions.'
The Sunday churches claim to be based on the truth; while actually thumbing their nose at the plain language; intended to deliver a plain message to the reader.

The first message to consider is about the correct timing of events. Consider how many hours there are (from Friday afternoon to Sunday morning). By making a simple calculation; I arrive at (24+12) **thirty six hours.** That is twelve for Friday night—twelve for Saturday (daylight hours)—and twelve more for Saturday night. The second message to consider is about the state–of–affairs which is clearly portrayed early; (daybreak); on Sunday Morning.

Once the two items are resolved; we can 'do–the–math.'

The notes above give us the apparent 'official' version; which is obviously a time period of thirty six hours. Please take a careful look at the real story and do your own calculations—to find a period of almost exactly **seventy–two hours.**

Jonah 1:17; ...And Jonah was in the belly of the fish three days and three nights.

Matthew 12:38; Then certain of the scribes and of the Pharisees answered, saying, Master, we would see a sign from you? But He answered and said unto them, An evil and adulterous generation seek after a sign; and there shall no sign be given to it, but the sign of the prophet Jonas.

Matthew 12:40; For as Jonas was three days and three nights in the whale's belly; so shall the Son of Man be **three days and three nights in the heart of the earth.**

The above passage from Matthew cannot be weasled away. Three days and three nights is always going to add up to **seventy two hours.** So what led to the Friday tradition?

It 'arrived' because of the reference to 'a' sabbath–day; (the following day). The confusion (for some) came from the fact that there was an extra 'holy–day' or Sabbath, during the week. More confusion was added when Bible translators (possibly under pressure) changed the word Passover to [easter]; thus disregarding the meaning of the text.

To help keep track of the days, we need to look back to the prophet Daniel, who lived in the period of the Babylonian captivity.

The writing of Daniel was in the period (approx 605-538 BC) Daniel: 9:27; And He shall confirm the covenant with many—for one week: and **in the midst of the week** he shall cause the sacrifice and the oblation to cease. So it is clear that the "old covenant" sacrifices would be (done–away–with) and the one sacrifice would take their place. We also see that it was to occur in the middle of the week.

The crucifixion occurred on Passover—the 14th of Abib or (Nisan), (the first month in the Sacred Calendar). This event occurred on a Wednesday in the year 31 AD!

According to the *Roman* calendar; it was Wednesday the 25th April. The time was announced as between the ninth and twelfth hours—which refers to daylight hours. Thus the time of death is fixed as 'just before sundown.'

The following day was a part of an annual festival (it was a day off and the shops would be closed). The Thursday Sabbath for Passover is the thing that caused the confusion (for those who couln't read or didn't care). Now counting forward three days and three nights (from Wed. p.m.) we reach Saturday p.m. (The end of The Sabbath Day) and the time of ressurection is just before sundown.

Now for the state of affairs on Sunday at sunrise.

Mark: 16:1; And when the sabbath was past, Mary Magdalene, and Mary, the mother of James, and Salome, had bought sweet spices, that they might come and anoint him. And very early in the morning *the first day of the week*, they came unto the sepulchre at the rising of the sun. And they said among themselves, Who shall roll us away the stone from the door of the sepulchre? And when they looked, they saw that the stone was rolled away: for it was very great. And entering into the sepulchre, they saw a young man sitting on the right side, clothed in a long white garment; and they were frightened. And he said unto them, Be not afraid: You seek Jesus of Nazareth, which was crucified: **he is risen;** he is not here: behold the place where they laid him] (KJV).

So for *any* reader, the message is quite plain—by daylight on the first day of the week, the resurrection was already over–and–done–with (the previous afternoon).

Those who attend a sunrise service on easter Sunday are following a completely false notion.

Alexander Hislop elaborated on the origin of easter (or astarte) in his book The Two Babylons: "It bears its Chaldean origin on its very forehead. Easter is nothing else than Astarte, one of the titles of Beltis, the queen of heaven...That name, as found by Layard on the Assyrian monuments, is Ishtar." In nearly all Semitic dialects, "ishtar" is pronounced "easter." Easter festivities extensively refer to celebrating the personage known as Ishtar, Ashtoreth or the "queen of heaven," who has many interchangeable (false) names. Each year citizens in pagan nations celebrate her son's death and return during spring.

What does the following sound like to you?—

Spring is in the air! Flowers and bunnies decorate the home. The children paint beautiful designs on eggs dyed in various colours. These eggs, which will later be hidden and searched for, are placed into lovely, seasonal baskets. The wonderful aroma of the hot cross buns waft through the house. The whole family picks out their Sunday best to wear to the next morning's sunrise worship to celebrate a resurrection and the renewal of life. Everyone looks forward to a succulent ham with all the trimmings. It will be a thrilling day. After all, it is one of the most important religious holidays of the year.

Sounds like 'Easter', right?—This is actually a description of an ancient Babylonian family—2000 BC—honouring the resurrection of their god, Tammuz, who was brought back from the underworld by his mother/wife, Ishtar. Throughout the centuries, millions of people have been persuaded to believe that easter's purpose is an honourable one; Yet this age-old global tradition can be traced back thousands of years (before its 'supposed' beginnings).

For the first two hundred years of European life in North America, only a few states, mostly in the South, paid any attention to Easter. After the Civil War; Americans began celebrating this holiday: "Easter first became an American tradition in the 1870s. The original thirteen colonies of America began as a 'Christian' nation, as such they did NOT observe Easter within an entire century of the founding of the colonies.

Chapter Thirteen

THE PATHS OF THE SEA

Please consider, while reading this section, the vast time difference from the recording of the text to the discovery of the scientific facts.

The Book known as 'The Book of Psalms;' was written by various authors. King David produced almost half of the material. The text quoted was recorded in the time of Moses (approx **1400 BC**). Science discovered the 'fact' in recent times. Also, if this text was supposedly written to please the "church" the person writing it may have risked being wiped out, (just for recording something useful).

[In the early **1800's AD**] When 'Matthew F. Maury' was confined to bed he asked his young daughter to read to him. She opened up at Psalms 8: and started reading, 'the fowl of the air, and the fish of the sea, and whatsoever passes through the **paths of the sea**' (KJV).

(See note by K. STILES; below). Later, Matthew was nicknamed "Pathfinder of the Seas" and father of modern oceanography and naval meteorology and later still, "Scientist of the Seas," due to the publication of his extensive works in his books, especially *Physical Geography of the Sea* (1855), the first extensive and comprehensive book on oceanography to be published.

Maury made many important new contributions, to charting **winds** and **ocean currents**, including ocean lanes, for passing ships. The following paragraph shows a little about the 'style' of Maury's work.

[This idea of divine order and design occurs again and again in the Book like the motive in a piece of music]. In fact, Maury was well read in the Bible, (quotations from which appear in his writings by the dozen). He had very definite ideas about the relation between science and the Bible, and declared that it was his rule never to forget who was the Author of the great volume which nature spreads out before men, and always to remember that the same Being was the author of The Book which revelation holds forth for contemplation.

It was his opinion that, though the works were entirely different, their records were equally true, and that when they bear upon the same point, as they occasionally do, it would be impossible for them to contradict each other. If the two cannot be reconciled, the fault therefore is in man's weakness and blindness in interpreting them aright].

["A Brief Sketch" of the Work of Matthew Fontaine Maury; By Richard Launcelot Maury 1915 AD]
The following text is 'The Introduction' to the above work:–

WHEN I took charge of the Georgia Room, in the Confederate Museum, in Richmond, Virginia in 1897, I found among the De Renne collection an engraving of the pleasant, intellectual face of Commodore Matthew Fontaine Maury, so I went to his son, Colonel Richard L. Maury, who had been with his father in all his work here, and urged him to write the history of it, while memory, papers and books could be referred to, this carefully written, accurate paper was the result.

At one time, when Commodore Maury was very sick, he asked one of his daughters to get the Bible and read to him. She chose Psalm 8, the eighth verse of which speaks of "whatsoever walketh through the paths of the sea," he repeated "the paths of the sea, the paths of the sea, if God says the paths of the sea, they are there, and if I ever get out of this bed I will find them."

He did begin his deep sea soundings as soon as he was strong enough, and found that two ridges extended from the New York coast to England, so he made charts for ships to sail over one path to England and return over the other.]

[The proceeds from the sale of this little pamphlet will be used as the beginning of a fund for the erection of a monument to Commodore Maury in Richmond].

[KATHERINE C. STILES.]

It is important for the reader to note that Matthew Maury did not give the tick of approval to all things; but to the words that were found to be truthful and accurate. I feel that his quote can work both ways... "If there is any difference between science and instruction "the fault therefore is in man's weakness and blindness in interpreting *them* aright."

(And this next fellow was once a Catholic priest).

The 16th century Italian philosopher Giordano Bruno was charged and then killed—for a stubborn adherence to his then unorthodox beliefs—including the ideas of the universe as infinite space, and the idea that 'other solar systems' exist.. Art historian Ingrid Rowland recounts Bruno's journey through a quickly changing Reformation-era Europe, where he managed to stir up controversy at every turn. Having a habit of calling schoolmasters "asses," Bruno was jailed in Geneva for slandering his professor, after publishing a broadsheet, listing twenty mistakes the man had made in a single lecture.

[Bruno's adventures in free thought ended when The Roman Inquisition declared him "an impenitent, pertinacious, and obstinate heretic," to which he characteristically replied, "You may be more afraid to bring that sentence against me than I am to accept it]."

In 1600 the inquisitors sentenced him to death. (At least his universe survived). [Ingrid D Rowland: "Giordano Bruno— Philosopher and Heretic"]

Besides infinty; the other thing that was feared by superstitious people; was the number zero. It just didn't seem right to need a number that represented nothing. This lack of zero held back the nations concerned for many years. (We certainly had no hope of a decimal system; no hope of modular arithmetic; and therefore no hope of electronic calculations—without the understanding of the value of zero.

And now a quote from a time when 'popular opinion' had the sun travelling across the sky. Exodus 34:21; six days you shall work, but on the seventh day you shall rest: in earing time and in harvest you shall rest. And you shall observe the feast of weeks, of the firstfruits of wheat harvest, and the feast of ingathering at the **year's end.**

The words "year's end" are translated from the Hebrew: (shaneh) {shaw-neh} in plura or (feminine) (shanah) {shaw-naw'}; **a year** (as a revolution of time); followed by the Hebrew word: (tquwphah) {tek-oo-faw'} or (tquphah) {tek-oo-faw'}; **a revolution,** i.e. (of the sun-course), (of time) lapse: **circuit,** come about, end.

Please note: The ancient (Hebrew) dictionary clearly links a year with a revolution around a 'course' (which takes one year to complete). And it had this definition thousands of years before the 'science.' There certainly was *no reason*—to believe that the sun travelled across. They describe the Earth doing a cicuit, this is very plain.

It's also important to realise that the hebrew calendar was a **nineteen year calendar** (Normal years had 360 days, leap years had *an extra month*, and adjustments as needed). Science later proved that the circuits of the sun and the moon coincide **exactly once every nineteen years!**

The four winds...
Ecclesiastes: 1:6; (The wind goeth toward the south, and turneth about unto the north; it whirleth about continually, and

the wind returneth again according to his circuits). The Hebrew for 'circuits:' (cabiyb) {saw-beeb'} or (feminine) cbiybah {seb-ee-baw'}; (as noun) a circle, neighbour, or environs; but chiefly (as adverb, with or without preposition) around: (place, round) about, **circuit**, compass, on every side. When combined with; Revelation of John 7:1; And after these things I saw four angels standing on the four [*quarters*] of the Earth, holding **the four winds of the Earth**, that the wind should not blow, on the earth nor on the sea, nor on any tree. Note; the key word here (and perhaps mistranslated); Hebrew: (gonia) {go-nee'-ah}; an angle, corner or quarter. So today; translate it to read; **on the four 'quarters' of the Earth**, holding back the four winds. The actual message was recorded thousands of years ago, at a time when humans had little knowledge of the weather (no high–flying aircraft) and (no sophisticated test–equipment)—yet clearly in agreement with something recently discovered by science.

A jet–steam is a narrow current of strong wind circling the Earth from west to east at altitudes of about 11 to 13 km above sea level. There are usually **four distinct jet streams**, two each in the Northern and Southern hemispheres. Jet–stream wind–speeds average 56km/hr in the summer and 120 km/hr in the winter. They are caused by significant differences in the temperatures of adjacent air masses. These differences occur where cold, polar air meets warmer, equatorial air, especially in the latitudes of the westerlies.

THE BOOK

The question of the Authenticity of 'The Book.'

Do we have a reasonable 'copy' today; showing the original 'intent' and the original 'meaning?' This section takes a brief look at what has happened to the various books; along the way. With these accounts; you'll find some ideas about what went right (and some things that were changed).

Many millions today believe that the Catholic Church "canonized" (approved) the Bible for our use. I hope to show a different case; (or at least encourage you to investigate further). The "pre-catholic" books were preserved reasonably intact. Only the 'order' of the books was 're–arranged .' By the time 'The King James Version' was prepared however the Book's content was still (surprisingly) as accurate as possible (considering translation issues and un-authorised additions).

Today's students will surely debate the official "age" of the Dead Sea Scrolls. The (200 BC) dating of these was determined by the type of parchment and perhaps by the hebrew characters used for writing. Also note that some of the [paper] was thought to be from hundreds of years earlier. It is important to see that the scrolls were being copied. The workers had access to a store of preserved [paper] and would chose according to what was being copied. The scrolls may have been stored away, (in suitable caves for preservation), any time from 200 BC through to 70 AD (and might appear to be from

NEVILLE WILLIAMS

an earlier time). After 70 AD; the Essenes and the Sadducees were not heard of much at all. Another cause for debate will be the carbon dating of some of the [pages] (some came out at 2000 BC).

The Book of Job was originally written around 2000 BC. Thus; an **original** [page] from the [book] of Job would be expected to show an earlier age, (when compared to one of the copies)!

From recent articals I see the Romans out to destroy the work. Also; note that the Essene Community itself (the ancient community that was being destroyed) was a community of Jews trying to preserve the scrolls. Note also that the Essennes may have been preserving the originals as; "backup copies;" but also producing some counterfiet [pages] to reinforce some of their own ideas. The Essennes had rules and laws governing their everyday lives in a similar fashion to the other groups; these extra restrictions were (ok) for them; (it allowed them to perform a task); however such restrictions were not meant to be 'peddled' as an idea for everyone to obey.

Whenever a 'genuine' copy was made; they would carefully copy the text (writing with [pen] and ink on specially preserved [paper]; then follow each [page] with a manual word count; and letter count). So we can see that most 'scribes' who were set apart for this task intended to work with great accuracy. (And some of them could not even read and understand the text that they were copying).

Two other groups around the same time were…
'The Pharisees' (who 'thought' they were somebody)
And 'The Sadducees' (the elite).

Some of them adding burdensome rules to daily life; without good reason. These groups would have been well defined and well known (at the time). An interesting point arises here. The Pharisees; who enforced their own rule of law (i.e. a 'burdensome' interpretaion); were named as 'Separatists.' The majority of the population would not join these groups, but they would certainly need to obey certain rules and laws.

Taking a look at the Old Testament we can discover that the 'content' (of the books) is fairly accurate. First, take a look at the definition of the word "Tanakh."

Ta·nakh or Ta·nach (tä-nä); noun. The sacred book of Judaism, consisting of the Torah, the Prophets, and the Writings; (the *Hebrew* Scriptures). Derived from the initial letters of the Hebrew names for the Torah, the Prophets, and the Writings.

From this we start to look at the 'arrangement.' We find that The order of the books was already upset by the time of the King James Version. For example one of the original "Books" carried the title "The Twelve." Or "The Twelve Prophets." One book enclosed twelve smaller books, (sorted by subject). Many [scholars] publicly acknowledged that there were 22 books in the Hebrew Scriptures. Here then; is the correct order for the Old Testament Books. We first list the books of the law, also known as the Torah or Pentateuch.

The Law of Moses (five books): containing;

Genesis; Exodus; Leviticus; Numbers and Deuteronomy
(Note that the first section, has not changed). The changes creep in for the second and third sections.

Now, the original order of the Prophets. (Note how some books have been divided and then sub-divided:
The Former Prophets (2 books):
Joshua and Judges (combined into one)
I-II Samuel and I-II Kings (all four combined)

The Latter Prophets (four books):
Three major prophets: Isaiah, Jeremiah and Ezekiel
Plus "The Twelve" (Prophets); one book; (consisting of twelve prophetic books combined into one)
Hosea, Joel, Amos, Obadiah, Jonah, Micah, Nahum,
Habakkuk, Zephaniah, Haggai, Zechariah and Malachi.

The third division; known as the Psalms (the Writings)

The Former Poetic Books (three books):
Psalms, Proverbs and Job

The Festival Books (five books):
Song of Solomon, Ruth, Lamentations, Ecclesiastes and Esther.

The Latter Restoration (three books):
Daniel (one)
Ezra-Nehemiah (combined into one)
I-II Chronicles (combined into one)

(Note; the original order is chronological).
Keep in mind it was mainly the order that was mucked up; the actual contents remained fairly intact; preserved in the Hebrew language; (as shown elsewhere).

Now for the order of the New Testament Books.
(containing 27 books in four sections);
Preserved in the Greek language.

Gospels (and Acts): Matthew, Mark, Luke, John and Acts

General Epistles: James, I-II Peter, I-III John and Jude.
They were intended for the general Church of God and not addressed to any specific congregation. They largely contain general information.

Paul's Letters to Specific Churches:

Romans, I-II Corinthians, Galatians, Ephesians, Philippians, Colossians and I-II Thessalonians.

Paul's General Letter: Hebrews
Paul's Pastoral Letters: I-II Timothy, Titus and Philemon

Other Writings of John: Revelation.

Revelation is from the Greek: (apokalupsis); {ap-ok-al'-oop-sis} Meaning: disclosure: [appearing, coming, lighten, manifestation, be revealed, revelation.]

The word apocalypse simply means, a revealing.

Now adding up; we find 22 books of the Old Testament and 27 books of the New Testament, a total of 49 books—representing absolute completion. Out of envy, the Jews (of the second century) altered the number of "their" books to 24 (by splitting two books)— to erase this significance.

Even in the face of 'many changes,' the Scriptures remain fairly well 'intact,' though the order has been rearranged; (primarily by the Roman Catholic Church, and following the order of the 'corrupt' Septuagint version). They also rearranged the New Testament, to exalt Rome. But again, this does not mean they decided or established the content! So; if the non—catholic book has been preserved for this generation, why are there differing translations and which is which?

We simply need more than one translation, because some 'loss of clarity' comes from world view translations, such as 'vultures' in place of 'Eagles'. Some translations are done word—for—word; some translations are from meaning to meaning; and then put into context (in english). Any method can cause problems if the scholars are language experts with pre—conceived ideas.

Looking—back at the Greek, (from my own point of view), is not always as successful as it could be. I am working backwards; from English to the Greek. A much greater step back; (towards the original intent); would be to acquire an earlier text, (assuming I could read the Greek language). The safer and more honest way to read; is to consider the context of any particular section. Sometimes the King James Version will have a word (or two) that could be unsound (e.g. corners) then another translation might make it clear. Many times, other translations get it wrong (e.g. vultures). The context; (of the vultures); is discovered, by knowing two things. The 'body,' is not a body that has died—or is about to die, it is in fact a body of many people gathered together. The bones being gathered by the Eagles; are dead bones (with no food value). As for the corners—the same word is used elsewhere—and is translated 'quarters.' As in the "Revelation of John"; chapter 20; "...And shall go out to deceive the nations which are in the four quarters of the Earth" (KJV).

As I have said, you do not need to be an expert in translation to be able to read and understand; you only need a 'desire' for the true picture; and it is there in plain sight. For every counterfeit that's out–there, there can be found an opposing explanation; (which is generally, one that makes a lot more sense).

Sometimes a simple comma can cause confusion. Also; the scrolls did not have chapter and verse divisions. (Division into chapters could break–up a story in an unwanted way). In the following; a simple comma changes the entire sentence... The comma, which follows a lead-in statement, "Verily, I say unto you..." was added and misplaced. It changed His entire meaning. The original Greek, (the language of the New Testament), did not use certain punctuation, such as commas and quotation marks. Translators (using their own discretion) added them later. The correct rendering is," I say unto you today [in other words, "I'm saying this now"], you shall be with me in Paradise." When rightly concerned about the context it's easy to see a future event; (which still hasn't occurred to this day); rather than an entirely impossible event. We know for sure that the thief wasn't going to float-on-up-to-heaven. And; since Christ did not condemn the thief, he simply assured him of a future event. He could not have literally meant the same day. He had obviously not yet died; i.e. The counting of "three days and three nights" had not yet started; and the Earth (where He was resurrected) was definitely not a 'paradise.'

The text found at 1 John 5:7 and 8; is a lovely churchy sounding piece, and trinity believers love to read it. However the lovely churchy text is as fake as a two–bob watch.

Actually added around 800 AD to directly support a supposed trinity. Transcribers who believed in the trinity could find no scriptural support—so they added some words to support their own bizarre belief.

The inserted text (the last half of verse seven and all of verse eight); is pure fantasy! Those who use these verses to support the 'trinity;' are either unaware that the passage was altered, or they *are* aware but feel that their use serves a 'greater good.'

Many Bible margins directly state the truth of the passage. For example, the New King James Version (margin) reads like this: "NU, M [versions] omit the rest of v. 7 [after "record"] and through to the end of v. 8, a passage found in Greek in only four or five very late mss. [manuscripts]."

The print that refuses to fade away:- In an earlier quote I mentioned the ten rules (commandments). Now take a look at what is recorded and then carefully compare it to the view held by the present–day 'churches'.

Matthew 5:18; For verily I say unto you, Till heaven and earth pass, one jot or one tittle shall in no wise pass from the law, till all be fulfilled (KJV).

Psalms 89:34; My covenant will I not break, nor alter the thing that is gone out of my lips.

Daniel 7:25; ...he shall speak great words against the most High, and shall 'wear out' the saints of the most High, **and think to change times and laws.**

1 John 5:3; For this is the love of God, that we keep his commandments: and his commandments are not grievous.

Yes, the book itself tells the church to keep His laws.

And if your church believes 'they' are the kingdom (right now)... also note; 1 Corinthians 15:50; Now this I say, that *flesh and blood cannot inherit the kingdom of God*...(KJV)

Now let's take a close look at the 'church'...

With the now strong ties between Church and State; the 'State' carried out the wishes of the extremists (inside the establishment); and in turn the Church gave the ruler of the day some level of credibility with the population. So at this point in time; The Vatican became the new kid on the block. Because of this power; (Church and State); the Empire remained strong for another two hundred years.

So, all those centuries ago, we see the Pope of the day; (along with some good folks to do the killing); not only gave us Sunday as (our) new rest day; but at the same time gave us the slaughter of anyone who dared to keep the commanded "Seventh Day."

The relationship, between the Roman Church and the other Sunday churches, can be compared to a Mother and her "disobedient daughters." The daughter churches were told to stay away from Sunday; to go back to the old–fashioned "God of the Bible." The amount of [other peoples] blood sweat and tears that went into making Sunday "their day;" meant the Catholics wanted Universal rights to Sunday—so that all Sunday–keepers would be Catholics.

Merely by chance; the Catholic writers were giving 'good advice;' to the other Sunday churches. What a terrible dilema for the remainder of churchianity. If they stay on Sunday they are treading on Universal toes. But if they turn around and run back to the original text, they would be all–but admitting that Sunday worship is a hoax, still leading to the ire of the Catholic writers. For them it's a lose–lose situation; with no backing down.

And finally, what does 'The Book' have to say about the universal church and her disobedient dughters?

Revelation. chapter 17 vs 5

And on her forehead was a name written, MYSTERY, BABYLON THE GREAT, THE MOTHER OF HARLOTS AND ABOMINATIONS OF THE EARTHAnd vs 18

And the woman which you saw is that great city, which reigns over the kings of the Earth. . (Well I can think of only one city where kings and presidents visit, just to been seen)

BOOT THEM OUT!

The well known presidential historian Peggy Noonan summarised mankind's history in this way:

"In the long ribbon of history, life has been one long stained and tangled mess, full of famine, horror, war and disease. We must have thought we had it better because man had improved. But man doesn't really 'improve,' does he? Man is man; Human nature is human nature; the impulse to destroy co-exists with the desire to build and create and make better."

People on either side of religion are confused about their own condition. Those who claim to be religionists have no respect for The Book, yet they claim to learn from the Book. To the fundamental religionists I say… "either read the Book and make the changes to your life, or tell your customers the truth about the way you operate."

Those who proudly claim to be athiests are only part–time athiests; they firmly hold their annual festivals and rituals without taking a second thought. Such rituals, when carried out each year, are in fact 'their' religion. To the athiest I say… "either give up your pagan rituals or admit that you prefer to remain steeped in religion."

A person from either of these groups would think I am strange, simply because I refuse to participate in 'their' annual holy–days.

The future will decide if our nation manages to eliminate these ancient; mysterious customs. It would only take a generation or so to achieve a good outcome. Let's hope future Australians will consider providing (and supporting) the best available education for students.

Do you want Australian students being taught absurd; (man—made); ideas that will have to be 'shaken off' as soon as possible. Let's get rid of these 'Wallys' from our world and make way for some straight talking and clear thinking.

Whether we like it or not, we learn and remember things without even trying. For example; I have never chosen to watch "Home and Away" or "The Bold and The Beautiful," yet somehow I know that a town in 'Home and Away' is named 'Summer Bay,' and I know that a person named 'Ridge' is one of the characters in the 'The Bold.'

When pressed, I know that these (facts) are from a fictional source, but such is not a priority. I manage to recall the above 'names' as easily as the name of the American president. The point is, my brain is not sorting the information by the 'reality' field. When students 'pick—up' the rubbish that is being peddled around the world; under the guise of religion; they tend to remember—and then pass it on as 'information.' The cycle of lies and deception goes on—unchecked. Whenever you hear some 'churchy' sounding words from someone, try to keep this in mind, try to see through the garbage, try to discover the truth. You've got nothing to lose—except a tiny chunk of your previous world—view. You can someday teach your children the truth about the way religion operates, to help them avoid the serious problem of passing on the virus. You or your family can someday play your part in booting out these false teachers from our world—for good! Doing these things will seem hard at first, but after a few years, the pagan rituals come and go without a second thought.

Many people today count the Bible as a mythical collection of stories from the ancient past. Such opinion is based on the nature of the religions of this world; rather than from reading the Book itself. If you think of yourself as a 'religious' person——yet you find my account disturbing in some way——try to recall the source of the information. The ideas presented to you in this book are NOT my own, they come directly from the pages of your Bible. You can either read the Bible; and believe what it says––or you can toss it aside and go to church––the choice is yours.

If you are one of the few people who find that these thoughts are truly from The Instruction Book then you should change your world view. You must teach the truth to your children; teach them how to discern fact from fiction.

A good place to start with young people is to explain "the Lord's prayer." Show how the meaning of this prayer is so very different from anything you could ever learn in "scripture" or "sunday school." The Lord's prayer is not intended to be remembered (word for word) as some try to do. It is about the *manner* in which a person should "talk." The differences between the actual text and the teachings of modern religion are so obvious; you will wonder why you didn't discover them for yourself.

Our Father which art in heaven.
(That means One Holy Father and He's not here on Earth)

Hallowed be thy name. (This name is important)

Thy kingdom come..
(almost the exact opposite of floating off somewhere)

Thy will be done.. (God's will––not man's)
On Earth.. (as it is in Heaven)

If you take an interest in God's law, the question arises should I join just any "Seventh Day Church?" Each of the false churches and their ideas can be easily checked against the words of the Bible. Here is one staggering example of how 'man-made' ideas can turn out so terribly wrong. (Remember, these are **their** words not mine.)

The Seventh Day Adventist is asked to believe that 'The millennium' is the thousand-year reign of Christ with His saints in heaven between the first and second resurrections. During this time the wicked dead will be judged; the earth will be utterly desolate, without living human inhabitants, but occupied by Satan and his angels. At its close Christ with His saints and the Holy City will descend from heaven to earth. The unrighteous dead will then be resurrected, and with Satan and his angels will surround the city; but fire from God will consume them and cleanse the earth. The universe will thus be freed of sin and sinners forever.

They say that the 'idea' comes from the bible, however one must "prove all things; and hold fast that which is good."

One can prove; or disprove their theory with a quick read of Rev. 20. And I saw an angel come down from heaven, having the key of the bottomless pit and a great chain in his hand. And he laid hold on the dragon, that old serpent, which is the Devil, and Satan, and bound him a thousand years, And cast him into the bottomless pit, and shut him up, and set a seal upon him, that he should deceive the nations no more, 'till the thousand years should be fulfilled.'

So the Bible teaches a time without Satan and with nations of people; (the ones who will no longer be deceived). While the Seventh Day 'church' teaches that "the Earth will be utterly desolate, *without living human inhabitants*, but occupied by Satan."

Surely anyone can see that the teachings of that 'church' are almost exactly the opposite of the actual text of the Bible. If a church willfully ignores the text, as it is written, it would definitely be a good idea for them to leave off the chapter reference! In fact they are replacing the word of God with their own man-made ideas.

I guess one of the most confusing words used by religion is the word gospel. There are stories of 'gospel music' or the gospel about a person, and so on.

There is one important gospel message; that is the 'gospel of Jesus Christ.' The average Sunday church will teach that it is a gospel about a person, yet it is NOT.

It is in fact the gospel of the kingdom of God. If the churches begin to teach the truth about a soon coming kingdom; right here on Earth; they would be in direct conflict with their own man-made idea of 'floating off to heaven.' So instead of the truth being taught as the most important theme of the Bible; it is simply given the flick altogether.

So, what about you, do you consider the gospel of the kingdom to be important? When you go to 'church' are they preaching about a man, while ignoring His message?

Matthew 4:23, And Jesus went about all Galilee, teaching in their synagogues, and preaching the gospel of the kingdom, and healing all manner of sickness and all manner of disease among the people.

Matthew 9:35, And Jesus went about all the cities and villages, teaching in their synagogues, and preaching the gospel of the kingdom.

Luke 4:43, and he said unto them, "I must preach the kingdom of God to other cities also: for therefore am I sent."

Luke 9:60; Jesus said unto him, "Let the dead bury their dead: but go and preach the kingdom of God."

Please note, the Book does not say "in heaven." It plainly says "the kingdom of heaven." Perhaps the message should be written as "the kingdom *from* heaven." It is very important for you to always remember, Jesus did NOT tell them to go and preach a gospel *all about Himself*, but to preach the kingdom of God. If the so-called "*representatives*" –here on Earth – were to suddenly feel the need to be truthful, they would immediately teach the same message.

And if they did suddenly get hit by a dose of truth, how would they describe such a kingdom?

Revelation of John 21

Verse 1 …And I John saw a city, coming down from God out of heaven.

10 …And he carried me away in the spirit to a great and high mountain, and showed me that great city, descending out of heaven from God.

11 …Having the glory of God: and her light was like unto a stone most precious, even like a jasper stone, clear as crystal.

12 ... And had a wall great and high, and had twelve gates, and at the gates twelve angels, and names written thereon, which are the names of the twelve tribes of the children of Israel.

Verse 15: And he that talked with me had a golden reed to measure the city, and the gates, and the wall.

16 ...The length and the breadth and the height of it are equal.

17 ...And he measured the wall thereof, a hundred and forty four cubits, according to the measure of a man.

21 ...And the twelve gates were twelve pearls; each was of one pearl: and the street of the city was pure gold.

All of the passages describe a city coming down to Earth.
Who would want to be floating around somewhere else?

Please note that (144 cubits) is the **thickness** of the wall.
The cubit used in this case would be slightly less than.
500 millimeters.

It's interesting how just one verse can lead to so many questions (and explanations). When you just go screaming through the verses you stand little chance of understanding anything. This verse about the wall has a great deal to offer.

It shows why a verse must be taken in context.
How, sometimes you can look to other verses to improve the meaning.
Why, at times, you can only make sense of the verse by looking up the original text.
It shows how studying one verse can lead to more questions.

What is a cubit?
How is it measured?
In other stories; why use a plan written in cubits?
Is this a measure of the height or the thickness?
Yes, all those questions from one simple verse about a wall.

In the past each region would have a slightly different cubit. In regions with tall people the cubit would be around 500mm. However, in areas where the locals were shorter, a shorter cubit would be used. Because of the variable length, a doorway could always be made 4 cubits high.

I am 1.8 meters tall, therefore my cubit is almost 500mm, and yes, my doorway is just a tad over 4 cubits high.

To measure your own cubit, simply place a tape–measure or long ruler on the floor so that the zero–end is against a wall. Put your elbow against the wall in such a way that you can lay the lower part of your arm down flat (out from the wall). Now you are able to measure from your elbow to the tip of your middle finger. That is your personal cubit–length. Now multiply by 3.6 and you will have your height.

Reading the verse in context shows that the three dimensions of the great wall are already given. (The length the breadth and the height of it are already given). Only the thickness remains.

INTRODUCTION TO
THE PRINCE...

The best preparation for children is to give them the ability to think for themselves. This current world is overrun with popular opinion and sensationalism. Yet there are literally hundreds of stories where popular opinion has failed.

Religion must never be a popularity contest. People who want to get 'churched' are looking for the biggest church or the one that says nice things. Things that *they* want to hear. If children can learn the truth at an early age they will instinctively know what to watch out for. They will know what it takes to find the truth. One must "prove all things, hold fast that which is good." If a church is saying nice things and teaching that the ten basic laws are "done away with," that will make them popular, but it will *not* make them a church of God.

Children who have not been inducted into 'churchy ideas' will find the truth much easier to understand. Once they have an idea of the big picture they will never be taken in by the false ideas that are passed on in the name of religion.

Even if they never read and understand God's Instruction Book they will be far better off without the false information from the popular false religions of this world.

For those who have made it this far, here is a brief overview of how we (as humans) arrived at this point. If you can read and understand a few simple pages, you will greatly improve your ability to pass on truthful information to another generation.

When you watch a news event; or even an information video; you believe that you are seeing both sides of a story. This simply, is not the case.

I guess the most glaring example I have seen, is a debate between a "young earth scientist" and an "athiest evolutionist scientist." After reading the Instruction Book, I came to realise that things were not as they seemed (for either side).

What if one being owned the lecture hall and both of the speakers at the event? What if one being had influence over both sections of the audience?

One group would walk away convinced that 'religion' has won the debate. Another, would walk away convinced that 'evolution' must have won the debate. The important thing to remember is that neither side believe in God; that is neither side believes what God says; each side believes only the information that has been passed down to them (from someone else).

A fine example of the prince at work is shown in a movie with the title "White House Down." Many people have watched this and believed they saw a movie about a young girl and The White House. The movie was actually about how the media behave in such a situation. Think back to the media's role in the events as they unfold. Think about which "side" the media was on. Were the media reports aimed at helping the girl? (and her goals)? Were the reports aimed at assisting the highest office in the land?

No, they were doing the opposite! 'Getting the story out' was more important than proctecting human life (i.e helping the girl). 'Getting the story out' was more important than proctecting the highest office in the land! The movie is a reflection of the real-world news media.

For today's media, telling the truth, (telling the whole story) is not an option. Sensational stories are made by a process of cutting out the truth and presenting a story that might please the 'majority' of viewers (out there in TV land).

THE PRINCE OF THE POWER OF THE AIRWAVES.

The god of this Earth; which we call Satan the devil; is also referred to as....

"The Prince of The Power of The Airwaves."

In the beginning was The Word and The Word was with God and The Word was God. These two beings are not alpha males (in the sky) as the athiest thinks. They have presented themselves to us as Father and Son so that we can understand that they are a co–operating family, The God Family.

These two beings designed and manufactured angel beings long before the Earth was inhabited.

At a time when the Earth became a 'life–supporting' planet, the angels **all** lived in a state of co–operation. The Earth was made as a place for some of them to live, to continue to co-operate and to make improvements.

That's right, in His Book, God claims to have designed and made millions of spirit beings *long before* He made man.

Billions of years ago he formed an atmosphere on **this planet** and made it inhabitable. The Earth was made beautiful and ALL the angels were filled with joy at the sight of it.

At that pre-historic time the Earth became the abode of one third of the angels, with Lucifer (the light–bringer) as their ruler. Lucifer was the most perfect spirit being that God could produce.

Lucifer and his angels were put on Earth to qualify as kings over the Earth (and eventually over the entire universe). To become kings, these 'beings' needed to remain obedient to God (and his laws) and to build perfect character, to prepare for *their* future as kings and rulers.

Lucifer did not have anyone to influence him; to lead him astray; yet he eventually rebelled against his maker. He decided that his way of competition would be better than God's way of kindness and co-operation. It may have taken millions of years but he eventually converted all his angels to his way of thinking. Lucifer then made the decision that the only way he could rule, using his own method, was to knock God from his throne and take His place.

Lucifer fought against God and His angels, but was defeated and hurled back to the third dimension—back to his life on Earth. His name was changed to Satan; which means adversary. Satan and his angels used and abused the planet until it reached the point described in Genesis.

Remember, the Book is not meant to cover the years between verse one and verse two; However it *is* meant to be a book for humans to read and understand. The Book rightly covers the period from the re-creation of the planet's surface, right through to the present day. There is also a great deal in the Book about the future. Reading about the future is like reading the news in advance.

The god of this Earth rightly sees humans as lesser beings. He would simply hate the idea of any mere human 'qualifying' as one of the many kings that will be required to rule over cites, right here on Earth. As explained throughout the Book, no human will float on off to heaven, no human will end up in an imaginary hell. But some will qualify as kings and 'rulers over cities.'

If any human can overcome the pull of this world and learn about God's rules and laws they have a chance to be one of the thousands of kings that will be needed in the future kingdom. If a person learns God's laws, including the original fourth commandment and overcomes the lies and deception, they may be able to qualify.

Even if such a person dies before that great day they will sleep in the dust and be called back to life when the time comes.

The false churches; ruled over by 'the god of this Earth;' teach the false (man-made) ideas of heaven and hell and the totally unbelievable trinity in order to decieve those who would seek the truth, and those who might qualify.

The true meaning of God's word is simple, anyone with an open mind can read and understand. The only people who would find it hard to believe are those who are already indoctrinated with the lies and deception of modern churchianity. It is because of the deception of the various churches that you need to give the little ones a truthful account of God's word, so they can recognise and avoid the rubbish that is being taught (by people who should know better).

At some point, the god of the Earth thought that competition would work a lot better than co−operation. He thought that he would get more done with this spirit of competition, (beings would become more productive). His method did not work and the Earth was damaged (as a result of the angel's anger and bitterness). His method (the get−what−you−can way) still holds sway over the people of this planet−−to this day.

The Adversary had no−one to influence him, (to make the terrible mistake of opposing his maker). Once he had made up his mind he became 'locked in' to that way of life, he can never recover. He eventually overcame all the spirit beings under his command (and swayed them also).

God now uses this Adversary as part of his plan to produce kings (thousands of them). The god of this Earth had no one to hold sway over him; and therefore had nothing to exercise against; he simply "flipped out." Humans however do have something to exercise against.

Humans who learn the truth about the soon coming 'Kingdom of God' have the opportunity to learn how to overcome the ruler of this world.

A person cannot simply decide to achieve such a thing on their own. One day they will hear the truth about God's kingdom and believe the things they have heard {or read}, this is only the beginning for them. To make any progress a person must continue to read God's Instruction Book. To make further progress from there they would need to 'seek' knowledge and understanding.

Eventually a person who reads and believes, will be called by God and given a chance to qualify (by overcoming the deception of this world). This will never be an easy task, as the world will keep dragging them back. People will drift between being committed to The Kingdom of God *or* being a part of the old world (which now appears to be completely upside down to the things they are trying to learn).

A person's "human nature" will often take over just as they begin to make progress towards the truth. This 'going to and fro' will happen many times before a person can finally settle for one way or the other; the old self (living in, and loving the world); or the new self (waiting for the King to come to His kingdom––right here on Earth).

The Instruction Book informs us that this 'Lucifer' character was named Satan after he was cast back to Earth. Lucifer was an appropriate name for him when he was 'with' God. His name meant light–bringer. His new name (Satan) means adversary. Satan is described as the god of our planet. He is the prince of the power of the airways. Satan is the original liar; the one who deceives the whole world; and he is very good at what he does. There has to be a purpose for all this, a purpose for human existence.

The simple answer is that humans have something to exercise against. We have a literal devil constantly bombarding us with his way of life. We also have God's rules and laws to learn and consider. By reading God's Instruction Book, learning His ways and then struggling against the false ideas that are so popular, humans can build upon their own character.

The Ten laws of God, in general, can be naturally accepted and obeyed, in our everyday lives. People who choose to join in with the 'churchy' are taught that all they need do is believe in God and they will be saved. Well what would be the point of that? One would end up being saved in a useless state. One would end up being God's adversary, obviously not a good outcome at all.

If you choose to believe in God, then belief in His Instruction Book must be included. If you toss out the Book, you also toss out your chance to understand what it says. Whether you believe in God or not, you certainly won't float on up to heaven and you certainly won't be dropped into any perpetual hell.

Life is certainly not meant to be a popularity contest, it is meant to be a way of improving **your** character and your children's character. But, just try believing God's word and obeying his rules and laws and watch how fast the rest of the world will turn against you.

If life were easy there would be no opportunity to build character. There would be no opportunity to exercise against the god of this world. There would be no chance for you to gain a position in the soon coming kingdom of God.

A SUMMARY FOR THE HARDENED "SCIENTIST."

There are two kinds of scientists, those who teach us to avoid the Bible, and those who use the Bible as a tool (to reach out to the population with 'known' information).

Higgs boson (example)

The 'Large Hadron Collider' has a simple purpose, to crack the code of the physical world, to figure out what the universe is made of, in other words, to find the God particle.

Jet–streams (winds)

Described in the Bible as the four winds in the four quarters of the Earth. The actual jet–streams were first noticed by airmen, during world war two.

Lazarus syndrome (a medical phenomenon)

Lazarus syndrome or (auto–resuscitation)
The spontaneous return of circulation after failed attempts at resuscitation. Such an occurrence has been noted in medical literature at least 38 times (since 1982).

Also called Lazarus phenomenon, it takes its name from Lazarus, who, according to the New Testament was raised from the dead by Jesus.

Ocean currents: (The Paths of The Sea)

The true story of Mathew Maury is included in this book.

The stars:

What are the odds of placing two accurate pieces of information in the one sentence, thousands of years ago? Please keep in mind that humans could only see a few thousand stars at the time. They certainly didn't have massive space telescopes to look through!

The Pleiades and Orion star clusters are described thousands of years ago when God asked Job a question, "Can you bind the cluster of the Pleiades, or loose the belt of Orion?"

It is only recently that science has realized that The Pleiades is 'bound together', while Orion's stars are 'flying apart.' The Pleiades star cluster is gravitationally bound, while the Orion star cluster is loose and disintegrating (the gravity of the cluster is not enough to hold the group together).

The Gyroscope (an aid for level flight)
Ezekiel: "The appearance of the wheels and their work was like unto the colour of a beryl: and the four had one likeness: and their appearance and their work was as it were **a wheel in the middle of a wheel**."

Ezekiel: "And when the living creatures went, the wheels went by them: and when the living creatures were lifted up from the earth, the wheels were lifted up."

My final comment is very plain and clear, (there is no wriggle room at all), so before I go there, I'd like to take the time to cover my own credentials.

What right do I have to read and understand
The Instruction Book? Or, what sort of person would qualify
as a likely candidate for reading and *understanding* the truth?

Gal. 6:3

> For if a man think himself to be something,
> when he is nothing, he deceives himself.

Luke 14:11

> For whoever exalts himself shall be abased;
> and he that humbles himself shall be exalted.

1 Cor. 3:18

> Let no man deceive himself.
> If any man among you seems to be wise in this world,
> let him become a fool, that he may be wise.

My first "full-time" job was with Telecom Australia, known as
'Postmaster–Generals Department.'
{I came sixth in the state in the entrance exam.}

I didn't get that job, yet I have been hounded all my life to "go
out and get a real job."

The reasons for not getting my first job are simple and
straightforward… (just like me).

This is how my doctor's certificate reads…

- He has defective vision. (I wore glasses)
- He is underweight for his age. (a poor physique)
- He has a history of asthma. (I used medication)

So you see, I am foolish and weak;
I am a simpleton, a blockhead.

And there are plenty of people…
(in the local area), who can back me up on that!

AND I FINISH OFF WITH...

A conclusion for the hardened Sunday-keeper...

First you should go out and buy yourself a new Bible.

Then place your garbage bin somewhwere near the exit door of your house.

On Sunday morning, get up and get dressed in your Sunday best.

Take your Bible out with you as you go, and pause near the garbage bin.

...

At this point you have a decision to make...

You can either go back inside and read the Bible –

or ...

You can toss that Bible in the garbage bin, and go on back to church!

The End